Does That Mean I Fail?

A Humorous Look at Pilot Checkrides

by

Brooks Black

D1571776

DORRANCE
PUBLISHING CO
EST. 1920
PITTSBURGH, PENNSYLVANIA 15222

Dorrance Publishing Co
701 Smithfield Street
Pittsburgh, PA 15222
Visit our website at *www.dorrancebookstore.com*

ISBN: 978-1-4349-3005-7
eISBN: 978-1-4349-2357-8

Prologue

About five years ago I was attending a Designated Pilot Examiner (DPE) annual meeting and we were exchanging stories about foul-ups on check-rides. We all had a lot of laughs and said things like, "Nobody would believe this," and, "Somebody should write a book."

I started this book about five years ago. I carried a small black spiral bound book in which I kept notes about the more memorable check-rides that ended in failure. Eventually, the book was full and there were notes regarding over 100 check-rides that had to be arranged by subjects and written so non-pilots would also understand what was happening. A daunting task to be sure.

I would get energized and write some. Then other things would get my attention and take up time. All the while my wife, Lena, kept after me to get back on track. Here it is 2011, and it's all written and ready for the editor and publisher. Unbelievable.

No one could make up the check-rides reported in this book. They're all true. I know because with only two exceptions all were personally experienced. Two other DPEs gave me one story each that were so good I had to include them. One involved cleaning of the windshield and the other involved forgetting to remove a pitot cover.

I have not identified any of the pilots involved in these check-rides. I don't want to embarrass anyone. My purpose is to provide some information that might improve future check-rides and have some laughs regarding the foibles of man.

I want to thank my wife, Lena, for pushing me to complete this book. I also owe a friend, Mike Leighton, a great deal for his assistance in getting my rough draft into the book you are about to read.

Table Of Contents

The Early Years

I had my first airplane ride in 1953. My Dad took my brother George and me by car from Toledo, OH to Kansas City, KS to see Grandpa Black. While we were there, Dad's older brother Uncle Harold, took the three of us for a ride in his airplane. I think it was a Cessna 170. Uncle Harold put me in the copilot seat and let me fly the plane while we were airborne. I was tall enough to see over the glare shield and had a great time doing turns, climbs, and descents. I knew then that I wanted to fly.

Then came the years of grade school, high school, and college. I managed to graduate in 1966 from the University of Toledo, Toledo, OH, with a Bachelor of Science in Chemical Engineering. Our department chairman, Clyde Balch, told us during our senior year that we would have three separate careers. The first would be in chemical engineering and the last two would not be related to our degree. But he was okay with that. He wanted us to know that the real purpose of the road to the Bachelor of Science in Chemical Engineering was to teach us to think.

After graduation I was employed by the Surface Combustion Division of the Midland-Ross Corporation. We built heat-treating furnaces and other process equipment such as gas generators and blast furnace air heaters for the metals industry. After a short indoctrination period in the design department I was sent out as an Erection Engineer. This is no joke. I was assigned to the Erection Department and my job title was Erection Engineer. All of us in that department had a lot of laughs about our job title. I was responsible for finishing approximately the last 10% of the construction of the furnaces and associated equipment, doing the initial startup, making sure the equipment operated according to specifications, and authorizing the final billing to the customer. Our nickname was, "chief fool." We were the ones that struck the match, so to speak, and fired up the furnace the first time.

We had to be very careful. The firebrick contained a lot of water. If the furnace was heated up too fast the firebricks would crack and the furnace would be severely damaged. The typical heat up schedule called for warming up 25 to 50 degrees Fahrenheit per hour until reaching 250 degrees at which time there would be an eight-hour hold. Then the heat up continued at 50 degrees per hour with another eight-hour hold around 800 degrees. We finished with 50 degrees per hour up to the normal operating temperature of 1400 degrees. This took a lot of concentration so we didn't have problems. We never left the furnace area. We would put a cot in the control room so if an operator developed a problem during heat up we would be right there. I remember an engineer who thought everything was going smoothly and left the mill for lunch. While he was gone there was a malfunction in the control system and the burners went to 100%, and in less time than the lunch hour the furnace was destroyed. I think heads are still rolling.

There was a very memorable startup of a furnace that was to heat titanium ingots up to a forging temperature of 2500 degrees Fahrenheit. I carefully planned for a nice slow heat up. The intention was to use only one burner at a time up to the 800-degree hold. The burners were extremely powerful and I was afraid of rapid heating. I lit the first burner and much to my dismay, even though the burner was still in the light off throttle setting, the furnace temperature shot up to 300 degrees in less than a minute. Holy crap! I had the furnace operators open all of the furnace doors and crossed my fingers. I was very lucky. No damage was detected and we just sat there for 24 hours letting the firebrick begin the drying process. We took a week to reach the 2500-degree mark. When we opened the doors at that temperature the heat was frightening. You had to take cover behind the heat shields when you looked into the furnace.

In 1967 several members of the Erection Department were sent to the Iron Range near Hibbing, MN. Our company had developed a process to recover iron ore from taconite. It was our assignment to build, startup, and ensure that the entire plant met specifications. Since this was a long assignment I had my wife accompany me and we rented a nice cottage on a nearby lake. On days off we went fishing. Frequently we saw seaplanes land on the lake bringing people up from the Twin Cities for the weekend. This brought back the memories of the flight with Uncle Harold and the desire to fly. We went to the local flight school at Grand Rapids, MN., and signed up to take flight lessons. Before students could solo out of the traffic pattern they had to successfully complete a dual cross-country flight of about 75 nm from Grand Rapids to a grass strip in the woods. The entire flight had to be done by pilotage at 500AGL to simulate the low ceilings that frequently plagued us. One day I planned and flew my long cross-country flight from Grand Rapids to Hibbing to Duluth, and back to Grand Rapids. I landed at Grand Rapids just before sundown in a very light misting rain. When I stopped the engine the sound of the instrument gyros spinning down was like a symphony. I knew then that flying would be my life.

I didn't finish my Private Pilot at Grand Rapids, MN. The plant was running well enough to turn it over to the customer and I was recalled back to Toledo, OH for another assignment. My father-in-law, Bob Perrin and I bought a 1939 Aeronca Chief for $1250. We flew it for 300 hours and sold it for $1500. What a mistake! I so wish I had it now. I rented a Cessna 150 to complete my private requirements and scheduled my check ride with an examiner, Harkness Davenport, who agreed to meet me at Fremont, OH.

Mr. Davenport ("Hark," to the pilots in northwestern Ohio) did my PVT ASEL, COM ASEL, IFR, and COM AMEL check-rides. He was a local legend and loved by all of us. His logbook spanned flight from Curtis-Wright Jennies to Boeing 707s. He had medically retired as a B-707 captain with American Airlines due to crippling arthritis. Once in the airplane seat he could fly without any problems, but he walked like Groucho Marx.

One of Hark's best stories was how he was hired at American Airlines. He and his friend had been supporting themselves by barnstorming. They would fly to southern Ohio and northern Kentucky on Saturdays arranging to fly over a small town around noon. They would stage a dogfight and inject oil into their exhaust to simulate a fire. Then they would spin out of sight, land on a suitable field and wait for the crowd to come out to see the airplane crash. Then they would sell rides. He heard that American Airlines up in Cleveland, OH was hiring pilots so he dressed up in his best Sunday suit, drove up to Cleveland, and found the Chief Pilot. After some talk they went out to a, "Big two engine airplane," and took off. Hark did some flying, and then they went back to the airport. On the first landing attempt Hark said he was too high and too fast so he went around. He had the same problem on the second attempt. Then the Chief Pilot suggested that he try the flaps. Hark had never flown with flaps. On the third attempt he was high and fast even with the flaps. He knew that if he didn't land he wouldn't be hired. So he slipped the DC-3 to a landing. The Chief Pilot said that passengers wouldn't like his technique, but he could be trained. He told him to go to wardrobe and get fitted for a uniform.

Hark could keep us entertained for hours. He told us about an engine fire just after takeoff from New York in a DC-6 with a plane heavily loaded with passengers, cargo, and fuel. A large crowd of spectators was at the airport watching the planes take off and land. So he had a large audience. He told the co-pilot to call the tower and advised they were coming back and told the engineer to start dumping fuel. They were able to land the airplane without any casualties. Another time just after requesting approach flaps the airplane began to roll uncontrollably. He knew that he had just changed configuration and suspected split flaps. He told the co-pilot to retract the flaps and regained control of the aircraft. He told us he was lucky that it was at night over Lake Erie; none of the passengers knew how far the airplane had rolled before he regained control.

His check-rides were always interesting. On my IFR test he assigned me a hold at an intersection defined by the BC-25 at Toledo Express Airport and a radial from the Waterville VOR. To make it even more interesting he limited me to one navigation radio. For non-pilots a Back Course (BC) causes the CDI (Course Deviation Indicator) to act in reverse sensing. If the needle indicated left you flew right to return to course. I attempted some pilot humor by thanking Hark for making it easy. I didn't have to realign the CDI when I changed frequencies from the Back Course to the VOR, as the OBS (Omni Bearing Selector) is not active when a localizer frequency is used. He harrumphed and told me to realign the CDI, "Just to keep things straight." This was an excellent piece of advice that I have used throughout my flying career. "Just keep things straight."

My most memorable ride with Hark was my COM AMEL. It was done in March using a Cessna 310C. It was a very cold day. We shut down the left engine and did some single engine maneuvers. I tried the restart without success. I followed the checklist exactly, but that didn't work. Then I tried some things that my instructor had showed me including a high-speed dive in an attempt to force the propeller blades to come out of feather. After 15 minutes of trying I told Hark that I believed the spark plugs had become frosted and the engine would need preheat to start. He said he would try. After 10 minutes more of him trying to start the engine he said, "Well, you need to make a single engine landing today so yours will be for real." We headed back to the airport at Fremont, OH.

On downwind I said, "Mr. Davenport, I have 300 hours and you have 30,000. Perhaps you should do the landing."

He replied, "No, you go ahead. It's your check-ride." On base-leg just as I was beginning to turn to final he leaned over and whispered in my ear, "Now don't fuck this up." Typical Hark. We landed and I rolled it off the runway. We put the airplane into a heated hangar. It later started without any problem. It was frosted plugs.

My daughter was born in 1969 and I wanted to spend more time at home while she was growing up and the travel requirements at Surface Combustion were too much. I found work at Owens-Corning Fiberglas (OCF) as a Chemical Engineer. I joined a flying club that eventually had 40 members and four airplanes, a C-150, two C-172s, and a PA-28-235. Dues were $40 per month and the hourly rate was $10-$25 per hour, depending on the airplane. We thought the world was coming to an end when the price of 100/130 avgas reached 30 cents per gallon. I managed to earn my flight instructor certificate, which at that time had the ratings Airplane and Instrument. I was able to teach in any airplane that I was able to fly as Pilot-in-Command (PIC). When the FAA changed the CFI ratings in the mid 1970s, existing CFIs were grandfathered to Airplane Single and Multiengine and Instrument Airplane if they met the requirements for each rating. The same logic was used regarding high performance and high altitude endorsements. If you had been doing it, then you were grandfathered.

I did my initial CFI check-ride at the Detroit, MI, GADO. (General Aviation District Office) which then was located at the Willow Run Airport.

They were not too happy with me coming there. They thought I should stay in my own district, which had its office at Cleveland, OH. The mileage difference was 40 vs.100 so I went to Willow Run. I did okay on the oral and also did okay on all of the maneuvers except one. When I demonstrated the procedure for engine failure at altitude to an emergency landing, I came in a little high to the emergency field that I had selected. No problem, I just slipped the airplane down to an altitude where it was obvious that we could have landed in the field. Just like Hark on his job interview. The Inspector said it had been a very good slip, but we should teach students to make the emergency approach using normal gliding maneuvers and the use of flaps. He told me to come back after I had practiced a bit. I was really mad at myself, as I could have easily performed the descent as he wanted but opted to show off. I came back the next week and flew to his satisfaction. Remember, "Just keep things straight."

I learned from that experience and scheduled my CFI-Instrument checkride at the Cleveland,, OH, GADO. I was to be tested by an Inspector whose name I think was DeSilvio. When I sat down at his desk he told me that before the oral was over he would convince me that I was wrong when actually I was correct. What a challenge to get started with! The oral lasted four hours. Among the highlights was the first reference book that I showed him, which was dismissed as a trashy rip off of available FAA materials. I did better when I showed him my set of FAA Exam-o-Grams for IFR. (Instrument Flight Rules). For the life of me, I do not understand why the FAA stopped printing these. I am lucky to have preserved a complete set of both the VFR (Visual Flight Rules) and the IFR Exam-o-Grams. They contain wonderfully simple explanations of complex topics and provided great rules-of-thumb for flying.

The Inspector tortured me for 45 minutes having me explain the most arcane information contained on an IFR En route Chart and several Approach Procedure charts. He grilled me for an hour on weather theory and use of available weather charts. After four hours had passed we were discussing various factors regarding aircraft speed, angle of bank for a standard rate turn, degrees per second of turn and turn radius. After he and I debated a technical question about turn radius, I surrendered and said he was correct. Then he smiled and said that he was incorrect, and I had been correct and that we should now go fly. I had brought a new Cessna Cardinal (C-177) to the checkride. He had not flown one before and was very interested in its performance and handling. He had me demonstrate a holding procedure and an ADF approach, then told me to return to the airport. I kept thinking, what had I done wrong? After we had landed, parked and shutdown, he said that I had passed.

Back then we used Flight Test Guides. They were the size of tourist trap advertising that you see in hotel lobbies. They were small enough to fit in your shirt pocket. The guides had all of the maneuvers and standards that are included in today's Practical Test Standards (PTS). The difference was that the Inspectors and DPEs did not have to accomplish all of the maneuvers. If the applicant did really well in the beginning he could have a short successful check-ride flight. Now all of the PTS must be covered and theoretically all check-rides are the same.

After I had my temporary certificate issued by Inspector DeSilvio safely in my wallet I asked him that if I had given up after three hours would we have gone flying then? He laughed and said, "Most likely."

I had some students at the flying club and gradually started getting calls from others. I started helping out at the Fremont, OH, airport on weekends. Eventually I made up my own oral test guides for each certificate and rating based on applicant reports about what the Examiners were asking. Back then the CFIs conducted their own oral examination of the applicants before recommending them for a practical test. Failure was not an option. It was a major embarrassment if your student failed and it was looked upon as a failure by the CFI if his student failed. Compare that to today's attitude, "I'll teach him to fly but he has to self-study for the theory."

One year around 7a.m. on December 24th I was loading my wife and daughter along with luggage and Christmas presents into the club's C-177, which was based at Toledo Municipal Airport. Hark was already at the airport preparing for a check-ride. I told him we were flying to Minneapolis, MN, for a family Christmas. He asked if I had checked the weather. I had, and I told him that my plan was to round Chicago before noon and beat an approaching front along with its bad weather. He opined that the front might be picking up speed. We took of heading west. As we proceeded we flew into clouds and began to pick up light ice. I asked the controller for lower, and descended back into the clear. Time passed, and we flew into lower clouds and started to pick up light ice. After the third such encounter I asked to climb knowing that the tops were about 8000 feet and that once in the sun the ice would come off and we would be ok. We made it up to 7900 feet. I could see the sun through the 100 feet of remaining cloud but the aircraft now had more ice and wouldn't climb any higher. I tried the roller coaster idea. If I could get up enough speed in a slight descent I could zoom up to 8000 feet. A good idea but while doing the descent and climb back up the airplane picked up more ice and I only made it to 7800 feet. I saw this was not going to have a good ending so I asked the controller for a 180 degree turn, lower altitude to get out of the clouds and clearance to the nearest towered airport with VFR conditions. He immediately cleared us down to 3000 feet and then cleared us to South Bend, IN. We broke out of the clouds around 4000 feet and landed. The FBO let us put the plane into a heated hangar to melt off the light ice that was on the airframe. While that was going on I filed a flight plan back to Toledo.

We finished the deicing and took off for Toledo. We were heading east so we would be lower than the clouds as the approaching front was a warm front and the clouds sloped up from west to east. Landing back at Toledo Municipal Airport around 1p.m. we were greeted by Hark who in his cryptic way said, "The front must have moved a little faster." I told him we had almost made it around Chicago but that in the future I would listen better to his weather predictions. He helped me transfer the luggage and presents into our car and wished us a safe drive to Minneapolis. We headed west on the Ohio Turnpike. As we approached the exit for Toledo Express Airport, I told my wife that by car we would be arriving in Minneapolis around 3a.m. on Christmas morning, and suggested that we just go to the airport and buy some tickets on United Airlines. So we did. The planned arrival in Minneapolis was 9p.m. We made it to O'Hare Airport where we were supposed to change planes. Unfortunately the storm got really bad and the airport was closed shortly after our arrival in Chicago. We didn't arrive in Minneapolis until late afternoon on Christmas. The moral of this story is a flying truth. Time to spare, go by air.

In 1970 I was promoted to Plant Engineer at the OCF production facility located in Berlin, NJ. I found a small airport in the area and flew on weekends. Occasionally I would rent a Piper Arrow and fly back to Toledo, OH, to visit. I remember one trip with a co-worker from OCF in particular. Somewhere over western Pennsylvania we encountered an imbedded thunderstorm. First the rate of climb instrument pegged at 2000 fpm climb. Who knows how much it really was. Then a large jolt and the rate of climb pegged at 2000 fpm descent. Then the cloud turned a green color. I was very afraid that we were going to encounter hail. I did what I was taught. Maintain V_A (Maneuvering Speed) and level pitch attitude until you get out of the turbulence. We came out of the turbulence unharmed and the clouds returned to a normal gray color. God was surely my copilot that day.

The Middle Years

In April 1972 I was appointed as a Special Agent in the Federal Bureau of Investigation. I was one of the last appointees to have his appointment letter signed by J. Edgar Hoover before his death in May of that year. The FBI Academy at Quantico, VA, was not yet open so we had to live in Washington, DC during our training period which lasted 14 weeks. Three other men and I rented a two-bedroom apartment in the northwest part of the city. Our landlord was a Frenchman named Louis (I can't remember his last name) who had been a pilot in the French Air Force during World War I. He was overjoyed when he learned that I was a pilot. He owned a Cessna 182 but due to his age (mid-80's) his wife wouldn't let him fly solo anymore. We had a great time on weekends flying his airplane. One time we spent Saturday at Kitty Hawk. During the flight to and from Kitty Hawk he related to me how he started flying.

During World War I he was a soldier in the French Army and was fighting in the trenches. Cold and wet he looked up and saw the airplanes fly over. He knew that the pilots slept in warm beds, drank champagne, and had beautiful women chasing them. One day some officers came to his company and asked for volunteers to join the air force. He was overcome with joy. His dreams would come true. The officers asked for volunteers to take one step forward. Louis and one other man moved forward. Everyone else had stepped backwards. One the way to the training base he learned that life expectancy for the pilots was about two weeks.

He was assigned to an instructor pilot who spent 10 days giving him ground school about how airplanes fly and the details of the systems and performance of the airplane that he would fly. One morning his instructor gave him a glass of champagne and told him that he would fly that day. His airplane was fueled with just enough to make one takeoff, one traffic pattern, and one landing. That way if he crashed, the airplane would not be destroyed by fire and it could be rebuilt for the next student. Louis was successful. His instructor gave him flight assignments and Louis would go out and practice. After about a week of this his instructor began teaching him about aerial combat. After a ground lesson they would go up in separate airplanes and practice the maneuver that had been taught on the ground. After a month of training Louis was assigned a combat mission.

He recalled that in the beginning, aerial combat was like being a knight from medieval times. You would fly out to the combat area and when you found the enemy you would fly up along side and salute him before beginning the dogfight. Soon after Louis started flying combat the tactics changed and the enemy would dive out of the sun unexpectedly. "The damn Huns," he said. Louis shot down several German airplanes, and he was shot down himself but was able to crash land in French territory. He was awarded many medals for his bravery and skill.

Louis taught me a lot about stick and rudder flying. When he was flying, the airspeed, altimeter, and directional gyro seemed to be frozen. He would be talking and pointing out interesting features on the ground seeming to have no attention devoted to the flight instruments. Yet they never wavered. His secret was anticipation. He told me to fly with a feather light grip on the yoke so I could feel a slight up or down disturbance, or a slight left or right disturbance. If I felt motion I should make a very slight response. It took some practice but I learned how to feel small changes and to make almost imperceptible responses with the flight controls. In engineering terms it was the difference between a feedback control system vs. a feed forward control system. In a feedback system you make changes based on instrument readings and then read the instruments to see the result of your changes. In a feed forward system you know in advance that a specific change in controls will cause a certain result. The feed forward idea is used by the new instrument presentation in glass cockpit airplanes. The altimeter and airspeed tapes have a magenta trend vector that shows you where the altimeter and airspeed will be in a few seconds based on your last control input. You must have an in-depth understanding of your machine to operate in the feed forward mode but it results in a much more precise control.

After completion of training I was assigned to the Savannah, GA, field office. My wife and I had just settled into a rented house when the Bureau decided that I should go to the Waycross, GA, resident agency. So we moved. Occasionally on weekends I rented an airplane at the local airport. I soon discovered that Bob (last name now forgotten), a neighbor across the street, was a medically retired Pan Am captain. He had lost his medical due to a heart attack. I asked him to go with me almost every time I went to the local airport.

Bob had flown The Hump during World War II. After listening to just a few of his war stories it became very clear that he and his contemporaries were true heroes. I remember him telling about a night flight, which required a refueling stop at a mountain airport. The runway had been cut into a mountainside and there were steep cliffs above and below the airport. On final approach his copilot noted that the runway lights had disappeared. Bob realized that they had gotten too low. So he went to full power and pulled up to best climb speed until the runway lights reappeared and continued the approach—all of this with the cliffs just off his left wingtip. Bob said they were too young to get scared. They had a job to do so they just did it.

After the war Bob hired on with Pan Am and rose to Captain. He was flying B-707s when he had his heart attack and was medically retired. He was a fountain of knowledge and helped me develop my instrument flying skills. His system was similar to that of Louis. Know your airplane's characteristics and make small precise corrections. He simplified the confusion about how to enter holding patterns with this: "Use the entry with the least amount of turns."

Another of his gems was what to do if you had flown an instrument approach down to minimums, had to make a missed approach, and were so low on fuel that flying to an alternate airport or going back to the initial approach fix and redoing the approach was not feasible. He said that when the ceiling and visibility are lower than minimums the wind is usually calm so timing should not be affected by wind/ground speed considerations. After the miss he would climb to 1000 feet above the runway and fly the runway heading for one minute past the missed approach point. Then he would make a 90-degree turn to the right followed by an immediate left 270-degree turn to the reciprocal heading of the runway. Then he would initiate a 500 feet per minute descent and flare just above runway height for his landing at the departure end of the runway. When I asked him about actual use of this procedure he smiled and said something about how it saved him on The Hump.

In 1973 after eleven months in Waycross, GA, the Bureau transferred me to the Kansas City office. We bought a house in Prairie Village, KS. A fellow Agent at the office who also was a pilot like me introduced me to his friends at the Independence Airport, Independence, MO. Gary Wilson ran an airplane repair shop there and between his employees and the local pilots, the airport was like a real life Terry and the Pirates comic strip.

The airport was owned and operated by Mr. and Mrs. Alford who were in their eighties. Biff maintained the gravel runway and cut the grass. Mrs. Alford ran the airport restaurant, which today would be a feature on the Food Channel's *Drive-ins, Diners and Dives* show. She was open for breakfast and lunch. On Saturdays she had homemade biscuits and sausage gravy. These were the best I have ever eaten. Homemade meatloaf and real mashed potatoes were another popular dish. And her pies! Homemade of course. My favorite was her warm cherry pie. She was like our grandmother. She scolded us for not eating our salad and then put more whipped cream on our pie.

I could write an entire book on the six years I was hanging out at the Independence Airport, but that might be a future sequel. For this book I will recount a few of the more memorable things that happened there.

One day an unfortunate pilot of a Mooney had stopped to refuel. When he was finished refueling and had restarted his engine something failed in the fuel system, a fire started in the engine compartment. Flames were coming out from the bottom and Big John, the chief mechanic at Gary Wilson's shop, quickly called the Independence Fire Department before going out with a fire extinguisher. We got the pilot out of the Mooney but the flames were getting bigger. The fire trucks arrived and the firemen went to work. One of them walked up to the airplane with a fire axe with the intent to chop an access hole in the engine cowling. He was standing at the right wing root with the wing on his left and the engine in front of him. By now the heat from the fire had started to heat the gasoline in the right wing fuel tank and you could see the wing starting to expand from the fuel pressure. Big John, in his typical understatement way of talking, went up to the fireman and said, "You might not want to be standing here in the near future." Then Big John joined the rest of us running for safety. The firemen quickly put a hose line on the wing to cool it and shortly thereafter the fire was put out.

There was a pilot whose name I have forgotten who belongs in the, "You're Too Stupid to Be a Pilot" chapter. He built a kit helicopter by himself. He was not an aircraft mechanic but he was handy with tools. As he neared project completion we suggested that he take a few flying lessons before he attempted to fly his creation. He laughed and said he already was a pilot and that his helicopter was, "Just another aircraft." We suggested that he should have a helicopter pilot do a test flight for him but he laughed that off with, "I built it and I will fly it." On the day of the maiden flight Biff told him to take his helicopter to the far north end of the airport away from everything for the first test flight. We watched him start the engine, do the pre-takeoff checks and pull up into a three-foot hover. The flight lasted no more than five seconds. He lost control and the tail rotor struck the ground. When the dust settled he was sitting in a pile of parts but somehow he hadn't been badly injured. Just some cuts and bruises. He said to us, "Maybe I should have taken a lesson."

One summer at the height of crop dusting season, a pilot near Topeka, KS, struck a pole with his airplane while crop dusting causing considerable damage. The insurance company trucked it to Gary's repair shop and the crew worked 24 hours a day to get it repaired. Then it was time for a test flight before returning it to Topeka. We decided to fill the chemical tank with water so I could also test the spray system. I took off and flew for about 20 minutes. I was satisfied that the airplane was performing satisfactorily and returned to the airport. The plan was to make a low pass between the runway and the taxiway and water the grass. When I activated the spray system nothing came out of the nozzles. The solenoid valve that allowed the chemical tank to connect to the spray system piping had failed. Now I had a big tank of water in front of me and I didn't want it there when I landed. There is an emergency dump valve to empty the tank. As I made my go-around I noticed that the shop crew and several pilots were standing ii front of the hangar/officer watching me. Evil laugh. I flew around the pattern and made a low pass at the front of the hangar/office and released the emergency dump valve with the intent of giving everyone a bath. I couldn't believe my bad luck. Surface tension held the water together in a giant blob of water and it was heading straight at the office picture window. As I pulled up to go-around I saw the water crash through the window and wash everything loose out the back door. Gary was very gracious saying that, "The office needed a cleaning."

We called the pilot in Topeka and he said, "Fly the airplane back to me and I will take care of the solenoid valve."

In 1975 while in Kansas City I earned my Airline Transport Pilot certificate. Back then you had to show the FAA your logbook to prove you met the experience requirements before they would administer the written examination. You also had to be signed off by an instructor to take the practical test, which is different from now as you can make the first attempt without an instructor recommendation. I was very lucky to have been trained by a TWA pilot who maintained exacting standards. He would allow altitude, heading, air speed, and navigation deviations of only the width of the instrument needle no matter what the conditions of flight. For non-pilots this would be 20 feet of altitude, two degrees of heading, two knots of airspeed, and one degree of course line. Contrast this with the typical ATP practical test standards of 100 feet altitude, 10 degrees of heading, 10 knots of airspeed, and ¼ scale deflection of the navigation needle or 10 degrees of the navigation indicator. Thankfully I had flown with Louis and Bob who had shown me how to fly very precisely. It was a lot of work but I managed to convince my instructor I was ready for the practical test. His final training problem was during a roundtrip night flight between Olathe, KS, and Topeka, KS. On the return to Olathe he allowed me to fly VFR, but had previously simulated radio failure so I had only one VOR navigation radio working. He asked me if the airport off to our north was Olathe. It looked just like Olathe should with the airport south of the city. I said it couldn't be because we hadn't flown long enough from Topeka. "Well, where are we Captain?" I told him I wasn't sure but give me a minute to think. I remembered from a long ago discussion with Harkness Davenport how to orient yourself as to radial and distance from a VOR using only one VOR by timing yourself through 10 degrees of bearing change while flying 90 degrees to the station. I performed the maneuver and determined that we were about half way between Topeka and Olathe and the city we were looking at was Lawrence, KS. He signed me off after that flight saying he was confident that, "You won't get in trouble."

I appreciated his tortuous training during my check-ride. The FAA Inspector that conducted the ride had me do a VOR approach on one engine with all navigation radios failed except one VOR. It seemed like the only time that two engines were working at the same time was the first takeoff. It gave a real sense of accomplishment to pass that check-ride.

In 1979 the Bureau transferred me to the Los Angeles Division where I was assigned full time duties as a pilot. While in Los Angeles the Bureau saw fit to provide training that enabled me to obtain a Commercial Rotorcraft-Helicopter certificate. Flying helicopters is a real blast. It's too bad they are so expensive to rent. I eventually earned the Instrument-Helicopter rating but have only a few hours in rotorcraft and do not examine in them.

I had a good friend in Los Angles named Boyd Bailey who owned a turbocharged Cessna Skymaster. We flew it all over the western United States during which time we learned a lot about mountain flying. One afternoon we were taking off from Mammoth Lakes, CA. The airport elevation was 7128 MSL. Thank goodness for turbo-charging. The wind was blowing pretty hard from the west causing some downdrafts on the eastern slopes of the Sierra Mountains. Shortly after takeoff I noticed that despite being at maximum power and best rate of climb speed our rate of climb was a negative 100 feet per minute, and the ground was up sloping underneath us. We prepared for the worst: An off airport landing. We discussed making a turn but decided to continue straight ahead for a better landing area. Suddenly the rate of climb indicator shot up into the positive range and we had flown out of the downdraft. Lesson learned. Don't fly when the wind is blowing hard over the peaks.

On another trip Boyd had to go to Laramie, WY. It was in the winter and there was a large snowstorm over the Rockies. We arrived over Laramie at 13,000 feet and were cleared for the ILS approach. At that time we were in sunshine but as we started descending on the procedure turn we entered the clouds and started to pick up ice. It got very bad very fast. I told Boyd that this would be a good time to use de-icing boots but the airplane wasn't so equipped. The crosswind was so bad that we were holding 30 degrees of crab tracking the Localizer. The window defroster was overwhelmed and we had just a small hole that we could look through. As we broke out and saw a runway through the snow, the tower told us we were lined up on a cross runway but go ahead and land. We decided to come over the numbers at 120 knots of airspeed, about 40 knots higher than normal, and use no flaps. I thought that the ice on the wing had changed the aerodynamics of the wing and was afraid of a high-speed stall. Over the runway in the flare at 115 knots the wing stalled and we touched down. The ice had come on us extremely fast during our descent and had not been forecast. Lesson learned. Always expect icing when there is a snowstorm. Later there was a radio call overheard from a pilot in a Beechcraft Baron doing icing research for the University of Colorado to the tower asking where the Skymaster had had the icing encounter because he wanted to fly through the same area. What a way to earn a living!

We went to Ensenada, Mexico, for some good fishing. The tower cleared us to land on Runway 13. As we came over the beach I commented that our groundspeed looked a little fast. We used up all of the runway for landing and stopping. After turning off onto the taxiway I saw the windsock snapping straight out and lined up for Runway 31. In the ATC office while closing our flight plan we asked the tower operator why he had cleared us to land on Runway 13. He said, "I knew you could stop on Runway 13 and I saved you some taxi time." What can you say to that logic?

Another friend, Mike Nesmith (Nez for short), was an Aircraft Mechanic with Inspector Authorization. As such he could recommend applicants for the Aircraft Mechanic-Airplane and Power plant practical tests. I worked with him nights and weekends until I had enough experience with him and

Gary Wilson in Independence, MO to qualify for the tests. There were five written examinations. Then he sent me to an old time A&P with examining authority named Al Misovic (I think the spelling is correct). Al was so old that he had been an A& E. You salute someone from that era. Al conducted a very thorough test. The first day was an 8-hour oral examination. The second day was inspection of both engines of Boyd's Skymaster and the third day was an airframe inspection of the Skymaster. Al also had little projects to take up any slack time. Pilots take note. Aircraft Mechanics are not knuckle dragging Neanderthals. They are highly trained and skilled professionals. They have successfully completed rigorous training and testing. We depend on them to correctly maintain and repair our aircraft. We owe our lives to their professionalism.

In 1989 The Bureau transferred me from Los Angeles to Headquarters in Washington, DC. I served as Chief Pilot for six and one half years. It was a challenging and rewarding position but after six years fatigue was setting in. The Miami Division requested a multiengine pilot to operate a Commander 1000 in the Caribbean. It took about two seconds to notify my superior that I would be volunteering for the assignment in Miami. My wife and I arrived in the Miami area in 1996. In 1997 with just under 25 years service I retired.

The Later Years

After retirement I hired on with a flight training company and became involved with training for the Embraer 145 regional jet, which had just received FAA certification. It was a lot of fun. Our office had seven instructors. Four of us were typed in the EMB-145 and we provided flight instruction in the airplane as no simulators had yet been built. Initial cadre pilots from various regional airlines were trained and tested in Embraer factory test airplanes at the main assembly plant in San Jose dos Campos, Brazil. We would go to Brazil for three weeks and be home for three weeks. Frequently my wife was able to arrange her schedule to stay with me in San Jose dos Campos.

On my first trip to San Jose dos Campos I was trained in the EMB-145 by two of the factory test pilots. Then there was a flight where I rode the jump seat as two FAA Inspectors type rated each other in the EMB-145. Then in a game of musical chairs they put me in the left seat. The FAA Inspectors type rated me and gave me examining authority for the EMB-145. So now there were three USA pilots typed in the EMB-145 and I was quickly put to work conducting EMB-145 type rating tests for the other pilots at the training company and initial cadre pilots from various US regional airlines.

I thoroughly enjoyed my time in Brazil. It is a wonderful country with wonderful people. On weekends and off days my wife and I were able to visit Ubatuba, Praia Grande, Ihla Bella, Iguazu Falls, and Campos do Jordan.

After 18 months of this I decided to start my own flight training company and landed contracts with two regional airlines in Europe to assist them in starting EMB-145 operations. I spent two winters in Sweden and a summer in Great Britain. The flying was terrific and I made a lot of new friends. It was great seeing places that I had only read about in history and geography books. Eventually my wife grew tired of commuting back and forth between our home in Florida and hotels in Europe so when the contracts lapsed I did not renew them and moved back home. Her big purchase in Europe was in

Copenhagen where she purchased a set of Royal Copenhagen china with a beautiful sea gull pattern at factory prices. Amazingly all pieces arrived home without a piece being damaged and we still use it on Easter, Thanksgiving, and Christmas. Yes, I wash and dry it by hand. We don't risk the dishwasher.

After coming home I began to conduct various flight tests in small airplanes as a DPE. In South Florida there are many flight schools that keep me and other DPEs busy. I also became an Examiner for the Jamaica Civil Aviation Authority (JCAA). Frequently a Jamaican pilot will come to South Florida for flight training due to financial considerations. Many times I will conduct a joint FAA and JCAA flight test for the student.

This is the shortest chapter in the book. Someday I might expand it with more details but for now this is enough.

Aerodynamics For Dummies

I suspect that some readers are not pilots and have no scientific idea as to how airplanes fly. Many of the pilots reading this book haven't much more of an idea either as evidenced by their performance during the oral phase of their check-rides. It is beyond amazing, it is appalling, to realize how little some pilots know about what makes their airplane fly. Some of the more interesting and hilarious examples are detailed in the, "Amazing Science," and, "You're Too Stupid to Be a Pilot," chapters of this book. What I hope to achieve in this chapter is to explain in simple terms that a non-pilot can understand as to how airplanes fly. If an applicant can provide some reasonable resemblance of what is in this chapter his DPE will be happy

Basic Concerns

Aircraft designers must deal with a lot of competing factors. The airplane must be fast and have a high climb rate. It must be energy efficient for good range. Production costs and maintenance costs have to be minimized. It must be safe and easy to fly. Most airplane designs are a compromise of these and other competing factors. For example, the airplane could be built very strong exceeding by many times the load factor required to meet government safety standards. The tradeoff would be a heavier stronger airplane with less payload capacity and slower speed. Designers must meet the requirements of Federal Air Regulations (FAR) Part 23 for aircraft with a gross weight of 12,500 pounds or less.

One of the first considerations of an aircraft design is stability. There are two kinds of static stability, stable and unstable. Think of a car at the top of a roller coaster. It is very unstable as a slight disturbance will send it racing down the track. Now place the car at the bottom of the hill just where the track starts uphill again. It will remain at rest at the bottom of the hill unless some force pushes it up the track. That is an example of stable:

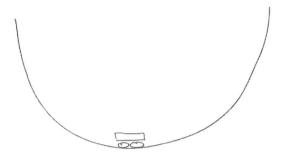

Static Stable Stability

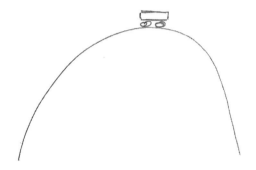

Static Unstable Stability

An aircraft flies in a dynamic environment. It is constantly being moved by turbulence and pilot control inputs. There are three kinds of dynamic stability, stable, neutral and unstable. If the airplane is dynamically stable when some force displaces it it will recover to the original state through decreasing range of motion.

Dynamic Stable Stability

If the airplane had neutral stability it would never recover from the displacement.

Dynamic Neutral Stability

An airplane with dynamic instability would oscillate out of control when displaced by some force. Engineers jokingly refer to this condition as catastrophic dynamic stability.

Dynamic Unstable Stability

Obviously the designers want the aircraft to be stable as well as both static and dynamic.

The fuselage design is affected by the size required to carry the payload (passengers and cargo), must have low drag and must provide reasonable moment arms for the engine and the tail. I will go into moment arms later in this chapter.

The designer can pick two basic types of wings, high or low. The high wing has a better lift to drag ratio (L/D) and better lateral stability. It allows for a shorter landing distance and better fire after crash protection. The low wing has better landing gear support; better roll maneuvering, easier refueling, shorter takeoff distance and better crash energy absorption. The designer can pick from a variety of wing shapes. An elliptical wing will have the lowest induced drag. A rectangular wing is the cheapest to construct but it will have unnecessary structure at the tips. This can be alleviated by building a tapered wing. A thick wing will have more space for structure and fuel but will have a higher drag coefficient than a thin wing. Another consideration is the wing's aspect ratio. That is the relationship between the chord line and the wingspan. A high aspect ratio (short chord with long span) wing is very efficient and used on aircraft like gliders. A low aspect ration wing is more stable and used on training planes. Most airplanes have something in between.

Cessna 172

Piper 28

The tail provides longitudinal stability and control and yaw stability and control. A conventional tail where the horizontal stabilizer and elevator are mounted near the bottom of the tail is most common. One drawback of this design is that the flow of air over the rudder tends to be blanked by the horizontal stabilizer when the aircraft is in a spin. Another popular design is the T tail where the horizontal stabilizer and elevator are mounted at the top of the vertical stabilizer. This design has good spin recovery characteristics but tends to deep stall wherein the airflow over the horizontal stabilizer and elevator is disrupted by the wing making stall recovery difficult. Another design used by Beechcraft for their Bonanza airplanes is the V tail. Instead of a horizontal stabilizer and elevators set at a 90-degree angle, Beechcraft used two elevons set at an approximate 45-degree angle to the fuselage. This design has less drag due to less surface junctions but is prone to a phenomenon called Dutch Roll.

Bonanza V-Tail

What engine should be used? It's a balance between how much horsepower is needed for performance and how little can be used for efficiency. Most light airplanes in the USA use some type of engine from Lycoming or Continental that produce between 100 and 300 horsepower. There are other engines used in light airplanes ranging from what we jokingly refer to as Maytag washing machine engines to Corvette engines but the overwhelming majority are from the two major manufacturers.

So you can see that the designers have a lot of decisions to make when starting a clean sheet design. There hasn't been a lot of progress in new designs since the 1950s. The big three manufacturers of light airplanes, Beechcraft, Cessna, and Piper are today building airplanes based on designs from 60 years ago. We have better engines, better materials and hugely better avionics but the basic designs are still being used. Cirrus and Diamond have produced aircraft of new designs using composite materials instead of aluminum. There is a new segment of light aviation based on Sport Aircraft, which has produced some new interesting designs. The future looks bright. Even though the designs may be old, they are proven. It is hard to beat the laws of physics. We who operate light aircraft will be flying airplanes with a gross weight of approximately 2500 pounds, having a cruise speed of approximately 120 nautical miles per hour and a range of approximately 600 nautical miles for the foreseeable future.

Cirrus SR-22

Explanation of Lift

An airfoil produces lift based on two scientific principles, The Bernoulli Principle and Newton's Third Law of Motion.

Daniel Bernoulli was a Swiss mathematician who was interested in fluid dynamics. He conducted experiments with flowing water and observed that when the water flow was restricted by a venturi, the water velocity increased and the water pressure decreased. Sir Isaac Newton was an English mathematician who in addition to describing mathematically the laws of gravity, promulgated three laws of motion. The third law of motion states that for every action there is an equal and opposite reaction.

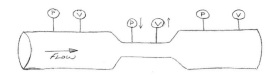

Bernoulli Laboratory Apparatus

Consider the airplane wing and its shape. For a normal wing (I don't want to get bogged down explaining special wing shapes in this book) the top is curved and the bottom is relatively flat. In front of the wing are molecules of air. As the wing moves through the air it bumps into them and they ricochet into other molecules causing a displacement of the air. As the disturbance moves further from the wing the disturbance energy begins to dissipate just like ripples in a pond after you throw a pebble into the water. If you watch the flow of air in a wind tunnel this is what you see.

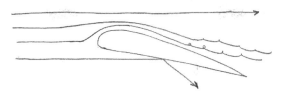

Flow of Air Over Airfoil

The flow of air close to the wing gets a big disturbance as it moves over the top. A little further out the flow doesn't get disturbed as much. Still further out the flow of air does not have any disturbance. It flows straight. Engineers call this a boundary layer. If you look at the top of the wing you will see a venturi formed between the wing and the boundary layer. Thus the Bernoulli Principle for lift. Air flowing faster over the top will have a lower pressure than the air at the bottom and the differential pressure will cause the wing to go up. If you look at the bottom of the wing you see air being deflected downward. Where the wind hits the bottom of the wing it is pushing the wing up according to Newton's Third Law of Motion. It is commonly accepted the contribution from Newton to total lift can range up to approximately 25% depending on the angle of attack of the wing.

For those of you mathematically inclined, lift can be described as follows:

$$L = C_L \times (\tfrac{1}{2}\, p\, V^2) \times S$$

L	Lift
C_L	Coefficient of Lift
p	Air density
V	Velocity of the air
S	Surface area of the wing

The coefficient of lift is a characteristic of the wing shape. We joke around that engineers use coefficients as a variable constant to make the math come out right. For the purposes of this book just remember that different wing shapes have different coefficients of lift. You can see that to increase lift you can increase air density, make the wing bigger or have faster air flow.

To have faster air flow we can make the airplane go faster through the air or we can change the size of the venturi being formed above the wing by increasing the angle of attack. The chord line is a straight line from the leading edge to the trailing edge of the wing. Angle of attack is the angle between the chord line and the relative wind. Don't confuse the chord line with the camber line. The camber line is a line from the leading edge of the wing to the trailing edge of the wing that is equidistant from the top and bottom of the wing. The camber line determines the wing's performance characteristics. For example, a high camber wing will look fatter and will be more stable but less efficient.

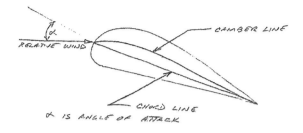

Chord, Chamber and Angle of Attack

As you watch the air flowing over the top of the wing notice that in the beginning it is laminar flow. A smooth flow. As it progresses towards the rear of the wing it becomes turbulent. The point at which it changes from laminar to turbulent is called the separation point. Lift is only generated by the laminar flow. Note that the amount of lift being generated is not equal over the entire surface of the wing.

Airflow Over Wing

Distribution of Lift

As you increase the angle of attack, the venturi being created between the wing and the boundary layer becomes smaller which causes the air to flow faster resulting in a lower pressure causing more lift. It also exposes more of the wing's lower surface to Newton's Third Law also increasing lift. At the same time the separation point is moving forward which reduces the ratio of laminar flow to turbulent flow causing a reduction in lift. Eventually the angle of attack reaches the Critical Angle of Attack, which is approximately 18 degrees for most light airplanes. Any further increase in the angle of attack will cause what we call a stall. This is where the wing no longer can produce enough lift to support the weight of the airplane and the airplane will descend. Note that the stall is dependent only on the angle between the chord line and the relative wind exceeding the critical angle of attack. Think of an airplane doing a loop. It can be stalled anywhere in the loop, even when inverted.

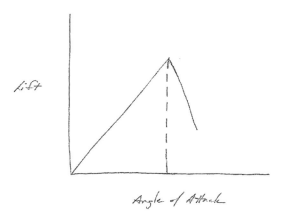

Angle of Attack and Lift

Simply put, if you want to make more lift make the airplane go faster or pull up to increase the angle of attack up to the critical angle of attack where the airplane will stall. This leads to an old joke in aviation. If you pull back the houses will get smaller and if you continue to pull back the houses will get bigger.

Drag

There are two kinds of drag to consider. Parasite drag is caused by things sticking out into the flow of wind. Examples are the landing gear, radio antenna, and boarding steps. Parasitic drag increases with increased airspeed. The other type of drag is induced drag.

Induced drag is caused by vortices formed at the trailing edge of the wing. Some people simply say that induced drag is a byproduct of lift. As noted above, the amount of lift being generated by a wing is not constant over its entire surface. Engineers like to keep things simple so the amount of lift being produced by the wing is plotted at the 1/4 chord point of the wing and is at a right angle to the chord line. The vertical component of lift is plotted straight up. If you remember your high school geometry class, you can prove the angle between vertical lift and total lift is the same as the angle of attack. The other leg of the triangle represents induced drag. So you should be able to see that at high angles of attack there is a lot of lift but also a lot of induced drag. The airplane is commonly in this situation during takeoffs and landings.

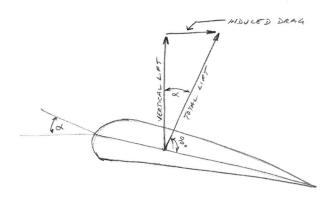

Lift vs. Indeed Drag

Forces acting on an airplane

A lot of you reading this are not engineers but for a short time you will have to think like one. Engineers talk about moments when describing how an aircraft responds to a force. A simple equation is used to calculate moments.

$$M = F \times d$$

M	moment
F	force
d	distance from fulcrum

When calculating moments for the aircraft it is considered that the fulcrum is the center of gravity (cg) and all motion is about the cg. Forces acting on an airplane are thrust, weight, drag and two kinds of lift, wing lift and elevator download.

T	thrust
W	weight
D	drag
L	lift
DL	download

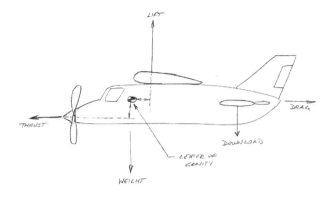

Forces Acting Airplane

The weight acts through the cg. Induced and parasitic drags are shown acting through the cg for simplicity. If you look closely you will see that the thrust has a lever arm relative to the cg such that an increase in power will cause the nose to pitch up and a decrease in power will cause the nose to pitch down. Remember that the thrust moment acts about the cg. Now look at lift. The wing lift also has a lever arm relative to the cg. Remember that moments act about the cg. Thus the lift is trying to rotate the nose of the aircraft down. This is balanced by the download (down lift) being generated by the horizontal stabilizer. Remember earlier when I said that one of the design criteria was for the fuselage to provide reasonable moment arms for the engine and tail. High-speed aircraft must be carefully designed so that the amount of lift moment being generated at high-speed will not become larger that the download moment being generated by the horizontal stabilizer. If that should happen the aircraft will pitch nose down, increase airspeed and could become inverted in extreme cases. This condition is called Mach Tuck.

Aircraft Controls

The airplane is controlled in pitch, roll and yaw. Each can be controlled separately and control movements are coordinated.

Pitch Axis

Pitch Axis

Pitching the nose up and down is controlled by elevator movement; to climb you pull back on the control yoke which moves the elevator up where the wind strikes it which pushes the tail down and raises the nose. This increases the angle of attack, which leads to more lift and the airplane will climb. If you push the control yoke down the opposite happens. The elevator moves down where the wind strikes it, which pushes the tail up and lowers the nose. This decreases the angle of attack, which leads to less lift and the airplane will descend. As the airplane climbs and descends the speed will change. Thus the pilot will have to add power to maintain climb speed and will have to reduce power to avoid going too fast in the descent. Another factor in the descent is that the increase in airspeed will increase lift. The pilot will have to hold forward yoke, or reduce power to maintain the descent. Pilots don't want to constantly hold elevator positions so an elevator trim tab is used. The elevator trim tab is a relatively small elevator that moves in the opposite direction to the main elevator and is adjustable by the pilot. If you are holding forward or backward pressure on the yoke, the trim tab is adjusted to eliminate the pressure.

Roll Axis

Roll Axis

Location of Ailerons

Raising and lowering the wings about the roll axis causes the airplane to turn. The Wright brothers used a wing warping system that caused movement about the roll axis. Octave Chanute invented ailerons, which became the favored design for roll control. Some large jets lock their ailerons in neutral at high speeds and use spoilers for roll control, but we are going to consider only light aircraft in this book. The ailerons work in opposite directions. If the left aileron is raised up the right aileron is lowered down and the airplane rolls and turns to the left. Think of the ailerons as wind deflectors just like the elevator. Some airplanes will also have an aileron trim tab. Nitpicker Alert! I am not going to address chord line change, adverse yaw, and adverse drag etc., until I explain the yaw axis.

Yaw Axis

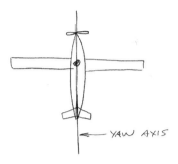

Yaw Axis

Movement about the yaw axis is accomplished with the rudder. If you push on the right rudder pedal the rudder will move to the right and the airflow striking the rudder will cause the airplane to yaw to the right. If you tried to turn the airplane to the right using only ailerons, the airplane would initially make a small turn to the left due to adverse yaw and adverse drag caused by the ailerons. The left aileron moving down would cause the left wing to rise due to the airflow striking the aileron. The down position of the left aileron would result in a slightly longer chord line causing more lift to be generated by the left wing which would also raise the left wing and start the right turn but would also cause more induced drag. This increase in induced drag would slightly slow the left wing's velocity causing the airplane to yaw slightly to the left. Thus the airplane would be turning to the right, but the nose would be pointing slightly left of the turning path.

Pilots control this effect by coordinating rudder movement with aileron movement. When the control yoke is used to move the ailerons for a turn the corresponding rudder pedal is pushed so that the rudder yaw overcomes the adverse yaw. The amount of rudder needed can be determined by looking at the turn and slip indicator.

Turn and Slip Indicator

The idea is to keep the ball in the center. If it is right of center more right rudder is needed. Pilots simplify this with a saying, "Always step on the ball." Most airplanes have a rudder trim that can be adjusted by the pilot so he doesn't have to hold right rudder during takeoff and climb. Why would that be necessary you ask?

There is a phenomenon known as Left Turning Tendency. It has three components for a single engine airplane. The component causing most of the left turning tendency is called the P-factor. If you carefully look at a propeller you will see that it has an airfoil shape just like the wing. What we call thrust could also be thought of as lift being generated by the propeller. The propeller blade on the down stroke has a higher angle of attack to its relative wind than the propeller blade on the upstroke. Thus the down going propeller blade will produce more thrust than the up going propeller blade causing the airplane to turn to the left.

There are two other considerations. The spiraling slipstream from the propeller will pass under the fuselage and push against the left side of the airplane causing it to turn left. Finally, the propeller is rotating to the right as viewed from the cockpit. Newton's Third Law of Motion, every action has an equal and opposite reaction, will cause the airplane to turn left. This is called the torque effect.

On some airplanes with high horsepower engines like a P-51, the pilot must set right rudder trim before staring the takeoff to counteract the left turning tendency because it would be difficult to hold sufficient right rudder to overcome the P-factor. On light airplanes flown by general aviation the pilot can easily hold the right rudder during takeoff and climb but will use the rudder trim to reduce the rudder pressure just like using the elevator trim.

Physics of Turning

When an airplane is banked for a turn the lift vectors are changed. Some of the total lift is converted to horizontal lift, which pulls the airplane around the turn. This results in the vertical component of lift being reduced and the airplane will descend. To maintain a constant altitude the pilot pulls back on the yoke, which increases the angle of attack of the wing. If you remember from earlier in this chapter this will result in more lift. The idea of a level turn is to pull back enough to restore the vertical lift component to what it was in level flight. This will result in increasing the total lift being generated by the wing.

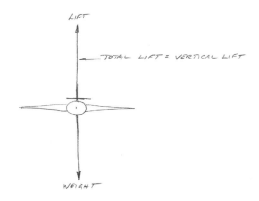

Airplane in Level Flight

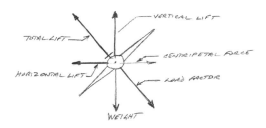

Airplane in a Turn

Remember from earlier in this chapter that increasing lift will also increase induced drag. When the pilot pulls back on the yoke to increase the total lift he must add power to overcome the additional induced drag or the airplane will lose airspeed.

There is something else to consider in turns. You can't beat the laws of physics. All forces must be balanced. Remember Newton's Third Law of Motion. The vertical component of lift is balanced by the weight of the aircraft. The total lift is balanced by load factor. Load factor is another way of saying G load. If you are sitting in a chair reading this you are experiencing a load factor of one G, the force of gravity at the surface of the Earth. If you go to an amusement park and ride a roller coaster you will experience more than a one G load factor at the bottom of the first drop and as you loop and roll throughout the ride. In an airplane as the angle of bank increases in a turn, the horizontal component of lift increases and the load factor increases. Most light airplanes flown by the public have a load factor limit of 3.8 G (normal category), or 4.4G (utility category) with a 150% safety factor by design.

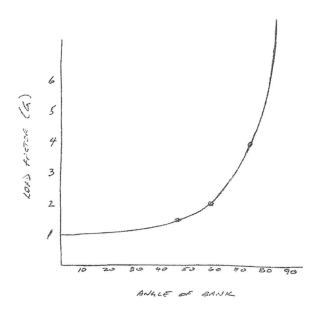

G load vs. Angle of Bank

Banking (Not the Money Kind)

When an airplane turns we say it is banking. Moving the ailerons will displace the wings in the roll axis. In a shallow turn the aircraft will return itself to wings level due to dihedral angle. The wings are not parallel to the horizontal. They are built to have a slight angle so the tips are higher than the roots.

Dihedral Angle

If the airplane is banked slightly by turbulence the low wing will generate slightly more lift than the high wing and the airplane will roll back to level without pilot input on the ailerons. This is positive dynamic stability in the roll axis.

In a steep turn the outside wing is moving faster than the inside wing. This higher relative wind speed will cause the outside wing to produce more lift than the inside wing sufficient to overcome the effect of the wing dihedral angle and the outside wing will continue to rise. This is called overbanking tendency. It is counteracted by a slight opposite aileron movement to maintain the desired bank angle.

Maneuvering Speed

Maneuvering speed is defined as the speed at which full abrupt control movement will not cause the aircraft to exceed its G load limit. It is expressed in aircraft manuals as the V_A speed. The airplane cannot exceed the G load limit at V_A because the wing will stall before the load limit is reached thus reducing lift and load. Engineers can determine the airplane's V_A by the use of a V-G diagram. As an airplane moves faster through the air in level flight it will produce more lift and more load factor. Through flight testing a V-G diagram can be developed.

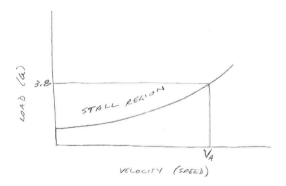

V-G Diagram

You should be able to see that below the V_A speed the airplane will stall before reaching the G load limit. Another consideration is airplane weight. As weight decreases so does the V_A speed. A good way to see why is to consider a 100-pound person being run into by a 300-pound NFL player. Then consider a 200-pound person being run into by the 300-pound NFL player. Who gets the worst hit? So if you are only given one speed for V_A in the aircraft owner's manual, it is probably the speed for maximum weight. You must then do a calculation to see what the speed is for your actual weight. Some owner's manuals will give V_A for the maximum weight and a minimum weight. You could then interpolate for your actual weight. Most single engine training airplanes have a V_A of approximately 100 knots.

$$V_A = V_{A_{MAX}} \times \sqrt{\frac{ACTUAL\ WEIGHT}{MAXIMUM\ WEIGHT}}$$

Equation to Calculate V_A

Spins

Non-pilots and many pilots are terrified at the thought of being in a spin. Spins can be a lot of fun. The best way to learn how to enter and recover from a spin is to find a good flight instructor. Spins used to be required on the Private Pilot flight test. The FAA was very concerned at the terrible crash statistics involving spins and in the 1950s eliminated them from the Private Pilot flight test. The spin flight training was replaced by ground instruction targeting stall awareness and spin avoidance. The program greatly reduced the spin accident rate. Currently the only pilot certificate that requires spin training is for Certified Flight Instructor with some kind of airplane or glider rating. The CFI candidate is not required to demonstrate spins to the Designated Pilot Examiner or FAA Inspector during his check-ride on the first attempt. If the CFI candidate fails his first check-ride because of stalls or spins, then spins must be demonstrated on the retest.

To enter a spin, first completely stall the airplane and then push one of the rudder pedals to the stop. The aircraft will begin to turn in the direction of the rudder. The overbanking tendency will cause the outside wing to roll over the top. The airplane will go through the inverted position and begin spinning in the direction of the rudder. Entering a spin is not the easiest thing to do. Modern airplanes are spin resistant For example, to spin a Cessna 172, one of the most popular light single engine airplanes flying today, the elevator and rudder controls must be held in the completely deflected position or the airplane will come out of the spin. In fact, the FAA will not approve utility aircraft for spins unless they can self-recover.

Standard procedure for spin recovery is as follows:

1. Power to idle.
2. Ailerons neutral position.
3. Full opposite rudder until rotation stops.
4. When rotation stops, neutral rudder and yoke forward to break stall.
5. Pull out of the dive.

Not all airplanes are certified for spins so be careful about what airplane you are going to use. The Cessna 172 is prohibited from spinning when loaded in the normal category. The problem there is that the center of gravity is too far aft for sufficient rudder authority. Remember moments vs. aircraft control. In light single engine airplanes you will lose about 700 feet of altitude per revolution. You will need about 700 more feet to recover from the dive. Don't expect to recover from a spin if you are a dunce and accidentally stall and spin in the traffic pattern at your local airport.

Multiengine Aerodynamics

Twin-engine airplanes have two additional aerodynamic considerations over single engine airplanes. There are two kinds of twin-engine airplanes, conventional and counter rotating. Let's look at conventional twins first.

A conventional twin has a critical engine. A critical engine is defined as the engine whose failure most adversely affects direction control. New airplane textbooks now say most adversely affects performance and handling. The critical engine for a conventional twin is the left engine. There are four reasons for this but when I learned to fly a twin only the first reason was considered.

The first and foremost reason is the P-factor. Just like on a single engine airplane the downward propeller blade makes more thrust than the upward propeller blade. If you look at the geometry of the twin-engine airplane you can see that the right engine thrust line is further out from the centerline of the airplane than the left engine. Remember that M = F x d. If the left engine fails, the right engine thrust will cause a bigger turning moment to the left than if the right engine fails, and the left engine thrust causes a turning moment to the right.

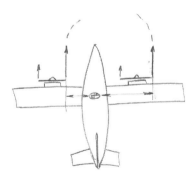

Multiengine Thrust Vectors

A second consideration is the accelerated slipstream. The air accelerated by the propellers flows over the wings and creates additional lift in that area compared to the rest of the wing which only sees relative wind speed. The air being accelerated by the right engine propeller down blade is further out from the airplane centerline than the left propeller down blade. Thus the lift on the right wing will cause a bigger roll moment than the left.

A third consideration is the spiraling slipstream. As earlier mentioned for single engine airplanes the prop blast spirals under the airplane and impacts on the left side of the fuselage. In twin-engine airplanes the right engine spiral goes into space while the left engine spiral impacts the left side of the fuselage. Thus if the right engine fails, the left engine spiraling slip stream hitting the left side of the fuselage will tend to counter the right turning tendency caused by the left engine downward propeller blade.

The fourth and final consideration is torque. Both engines are rotating to the right when viewed from the cockpit. It is an equal and opposite reaction. The torque will cause the airplane to turn left. If the right engine fails the torque from the left engine will be opposite to the effect of the left engine propeller downward blade.

The second, third and fourth reasons border on mental masturbation. Listen to the old timers. I mean the WWII pilots from whom pilots of my generation learned to fly. They knew about two, three, and four but discounted any meaningful effect on twin-engine airplane control when operating single engine. It was all P-factor. I knew an old airline pilot who had his own definition of critical engine. To him, if he were in the middle of the Atlantic Ocean the critical engine was the one still running.

The second consideration is velocity of minimum control. (V_{mc}) This is the slowest speed that you can maintain directional control with the critical engine failed. Aircraft manufacturers determine the speed by flight-testing. The FAA requires certain conditions for the test. The aircraft test requirements are maximum takeoff weight, center of gravity at the aft limit, landing gear up, wing flaps and cowl flaps in their takeoff position, critical engine wind milling, the other engine at full power, no more than 5^0 of bank—no more than 150 pounds of rudder pressure and the speed calculated for a Standard Day at sea level.

Why the limitation on degrees of bank? Look at the following two diagrams of airplanes operating on one engine. The aircraft on the left does not use ailerons. The aircraft will crab off to the left front. The relative wind will streamline past the rudder. The aircraft on the right uses sufficient aileron input to fly a straight ground track. The relative wind impacts the rudder at an angle making it more effective than the rudder on the left airplane.

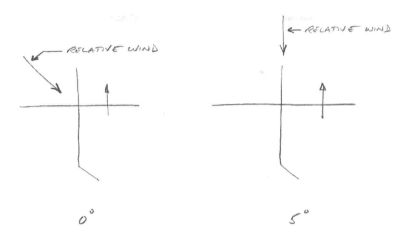

Effect of Bank On V_{MC}

On a multiengine flight test the applicant must demonstrate V_{mc}. The usual procedure is to have the airplane in the clean configuration (gear and flaps up) and retard both throttles. When the speed has slowed to approximately the best rate of climb speed the critical engine power is reduced to idle and the other engine is placed at full power. Heading is maintained with the rudder. Then the pitch is slowly increased until the aircraft begins to lose directional control at which point the engine power is reduced to idle and the aircraft is pitched down. When the aircraft is under control the power is then increased back to cruise power.

You must be aware that the speed of V_{mc} changes with density altitude. As the airplane climbs to a higher altitude the engines produce less power. V_{mc} is a function of engine power so it will decrease with increase in density altitude. It could become slower than stall speed. If you were doing a V_{mc} demonstration and allowed the airplane to stall first, the airplane would promptly enter into a spin. Remember how to enter a spin? Stall with full rudder deflection. The FAA does not require that manufacturers spin test twin-engine airplanes, so most have not been spin tested. Don't tempt fate. If you detect an impending stall while doing a V_{mc} demonstration, abandon the maneuver. Recover the airplane. Then the Designated Pilot Examiner most likely will have you repeat the demonstration using less aileron and/or rudder input that should keep V_{mc} faster than stall speed.

Some of the newer twin-engine airplanes have counter-rotating engines. The right engine rotates counterclockwise. Thus the thrust line for both engines is the same distance from the airplane centerline and there is no critical engine. Or do you have two critical engines?

This concludes the simple version of how airplanes fly. For further reading I suggest the following books. You can find them at most pilot shops.

EAA Pilots Handbook of Aeronautical Knowledge
EAA Flight Training Handbook
Aerodynamics for Naval Aviators

Amazing Science

It is truly amazing listening to some of the applicants 'scientific explanations' regarding aerodynamics, navigation, weather, and aircraft design. Some of the more memorable are provided for your enjoyment.

Navigation

Magnetic Variation

A private pilot applicant explained that magnetic variation was caused by the Earth's rotation. His explained that due to the rotation of the Earth, the gravitational field of the earth caused the magnetic field to bend and since the magnetic compass always aligns itself with the lines of magnetic force the compass would not point to north because of the bending of the magnetic field.

Another private pilot applicant thought that magnetic variation was due to the axis of the Earth being tilted. He was amazed when I told him that the tilted axis was the reason for the four seasons and the reversal of the seasons between the North and South hemispheres, not magnetic variation.

A commercial applicant thought that magnetic variation was shown on the Sectional Chart because the world is a three dimensional sphere and the two dimensional chart is flat. He gave a lengthy explanation how a three dimensional sphere could not be accurately shown on a two dimensional chart and how that fact resulted in charts for higher latitudes not being dimensionally accurate which was the reason for magnetic variation.

Another commercial applicant thought the difference between true north and magnetic north was due to the earth's rotation causing the magnetic north pole to move around. This also explained why some instrument approach charts showed the annual change in variation at the airport.

A flight instructor applicant just shrugged his shoulders and said he had no idea.

These are typical of about half of the applicants who just don't know that magnetic variation is due to the fact that the magnetic north and south poles are not in the same geographical location as the true north and south poles and that the variation is sometimes influenced by local disturbances such as the iron ore deposits in northern Minnesota.

Global Positioning System (GPS)

The GPS provides a very accurate means to know your position and navigate your airplane. There is a constellation of 30 satellites orbiting the Earth each emitting a specified time signal that the receiver onboard the airplane uses to determine its position relative to the satellite. In order to accurately navigate you must receive signals from five satellites, or if you manually enter the barometric pressure into the receiver, then you can navigate with only four satellites. GPS instrument approach procedures have become commonplace in the United States. Some GPS receivers have a vertical navigation capability, which allows an ILS like approach with lateral and vertical guidance. Some of these GPS approaches contain a limitation that Barometric Vertical Navigation (Barometric VNAV) is prohibited when the temperature is less than -15 degrees Celsius. The reason is that the barometric pressure setting provided by ATC is not corrected for temperature and in cold weather the airplane's true altitude is below the indicated altitude. The error becomes more pronounced as the temperature becomes colder (See Altimeter Setting Procedures in Chapter Seven of the Aeronautical Information Manual). In addition, the VNAV glide-slope angle calculated by the GPS receiver will be incorrect.

Now enter the Nobel Prize wannabe. An applicant for an Instrument Airplane rating told me that the reason for the cold temperature limitation was that cold air is denser than warm air and that in cold air the signal from the GPS satellite would take longer to travel from the satellite to the airplane's GPS receiver than it would in warm air. This would make it impossible for the GPS receiver to accurately know its position and thus it would not be suitable for navigation.

Aerodynamics

Production of Lift

Well-prepared applicants explain lift is due to Bernoulli's principle and Newton's third law of motion. They can explain both ideas and how both produce lift. Chord line, relative wind, angle of attack and relative wind speed are used to describe how lift is produced by a wing. Some of the better students discuss boundary layers, laminar vs. turbulent flow and the relationship between angle of attack, lift, wing loading and induced drag.

A very popular "amazing science" explanation as to how a wing produces lift goes something like this: Moe and Joe are two air molecules that encounter the leading edge of the wing. Moe goes over the top of the wing, which is a longer distance than Joe travels going under the wing. Since they must meet at the back of the wing, Moe must go faster to meet up with Joe. Due to the Bernoulli principle that says a fluid traveling faster has lower pressure, there is lower pressure on the top of the wing. High pressure seeks low pressure so the high pressure on the bottom of the wing pushes the wing upwards creating what is called lift.

This theory of lift is easily discredited by asking the applicant how their theory explains the flight of a symmetrical wing. Moe and Joe have the same distance to travel. Another good question is what scientific principle requires the two air molecules to rejoin at the training edge of the wing. I can understand a private applicant confusing Bernoulli, Newton and hangar talk but too many flight instructor candidates spew this drivel.

One of the best "amazing science" theories of lift I have heard went something like this: Nature abhors a vacuum. Because the top of the wing is curved, the air passing over the top is accelerated with a resulting low pressure due to the Bernoulli principle. As the wing moves through the air the higher-pressure air on the bottom tries to replace the lower pressure air on the top. This leaves a void on the bottom of the wing, a vacuum. Thus a ring of air begins to flow downward from above the wing to replace the bottom air trying to replace the top air. As this ring of descending air passes beneath the wing it changes direction to replace the bottom air pushing up on the bottom of the wing creating lift. I was stunned. I asked the flight instructor applicant where he had read this explanation of lift. He said he hadn't read it. The explanation was the result of his scientific thinking. His pink slip made a quick appearance.

Almost as interesting was this explanation of lift from a CFI AME candidate. Air molecules are accelerated around the top curvature of the leading edge of the wing due to centrifugal force, thus gaining speed vs. the slower moving molecules on the bottom of the wing. The speed differential causes a lower pressure on the top of the wing according to the Bernoulli principle resulting in an upward force that we call lift.

A private pilot applicant had this idea about lift. Air is going slower over the top of the wing causing lower pressure when compared to the bottom of the wing where the air is going faster. The faster air flow at the bottom of the wing results in the air molecules being packed denser making a higher pressure which pushes the wing up with a force that is called lift. Absolutely amazing.

A CFI-ASE applicant had this idea about lift. As the wing moves through the air, air is deflected down by the bottom of the wing. The air flowing over the top comes off the trailing edge of the wing and curves downward. This is called downwash. As both streams of air bump into an air wall beneath the wing they are pushed back up due to Newton's Third Law of Motion and this pushed up air causes the wing to be pushed up and this is the lift.

Multiengine Aerodynamics

A CFI-AME candidate was explaining V_{MC} aerodynamics. For non-pilot information, this is the speed at which directional control of a twin-engine airplane cannot be maintained when operating with the critical engine inoperative. Aircraft manufacturers are required to determine this speed by flight-testing. The flight test has several parameters set forth by FAA certification regulations. The parameters for determining the speed include aircraft at maximum takeoff weight, the center of gravity located at the aft limit, the critical engine wind milling, the operative engine developing maximum power, landing gear retracted, flaps in their takeoff position, up to five degrees of bank, up to 150 pounds of rudder pressure, and a standard day which is defined as 29.92 inches of mercury pressure and 15 degrees Celsius temperature at sea level. The flight test is conducted at a safe altitude and the data is massaged to calculate the V_{MC} speed at sea level on a standard day and this speed is marked on the airspeed indicator with a red line On a typical twin engine training airplane such as the Piper Seminole the V_{MC} speed is 56 knots.

This applicant explained that the flight test was done with aft center of gravity because that would require the most power to maintain flight. He continued that aft center of gravity makes the tail fly low and the extra power is needed to pull the nose down. He concluded that the horizontal stabilizer was needed to provide additional lift to keep the tail up when there is aft center of gravity. This applicant had no idea as to how the horizontal stabilizer provides a down force to balance the lift being produced by the wing and that an aft center of gravity will cause the aircraft to fly at a lower angle of attack (nose low) which is more efficient due to less induced drag. He also missed the fact that an aft center of gravity will result in a short arm from the center of gravity to the rudder making the rudder less effective and that this would cause an increase in the V_{MC} speed.

Another CFI-AME applicant had this explanation as to why the left engine is the critical engine in a conventional twin-engine airplane. P-factor is caused by the downward propeller blade moving more air than the upward blade. The left engine downward blade is closer to the fuselage than the downward blade on the right engine. The air from the left engine downward blade pushes against the fuselage causing the airplane to turn left. The air from the right engine downward blade just dissipates into the atmosphere.

Performing Maneuvers

A large number of CFI candidates tell me that the reason chandelles are performed into the wind is to obtain better climb performance. They are speechless when I ask them how does the airplane know if it is traveling upwind or downwind. This lack of knowledge reminds me of the 'dangerous downwind turn in the traffic pattern' lunacy that was popular back in the 1970s. I remember popular flying magazines having articles citing 'scientific proof' of the dangers of making a downwind turn in the pattern. How dumb can you be? The airplane responds to relative wind. It doesn't matter if it's upwind or downwind. What was really happening was as the airplane turned from upwind to downwind in the traffic pattern, the groundspeed increased giving a visual illusion of going faster, causing the pilot to pull up on the yoke to make the sight picture look right, thus increasing the angle of attack. Occasionally the critical angle of attack was reached and the wing stalled. Frequently the hapless pilot wasn't paying attention to his coordination and the aircraft entered a low level spin with fatal consequences. As for the chandelle question, the reason the chandelles are performed into the wind is to keep the aircraft in the practice area (See: *The EAA Flight Training Handbook*) The only difference in going upwind vs. downwind would be more altitude gained in a shorter ground distance.

A CFI-AME candidate was demonstrating a single engine approach and allowed the airplane to become dangerously low on final approach. He explained that, "The reason we were low on the approach was I used too much rudder." I asked him to explain how too much rudder could cause the low approach and received this explanation. "Too much rudder would cause a side slip that would reduce the lift being produced by the wings and the airplane would descend." He never grasped the fact that he had allowed the speed to decay into the backside of the power curve and had the power setting for the operating engine too low, resulting in a high descent rate.

A CFI candidate advised that you had to add power during a steep turn to force more airflow over the wing to compensate for the loss of lift in the turn. Another candidate who didn't understand the relationship between angle of attack, lift and induced drag.

Aircraft Design

Aircraft Systems

A commercial pilot airplane multiengine land (COM AMEL) applicant was asked to explain the use of the autopilot installed in the test aircraft. He said he never used the autopilot because it could damage the airplane. I asked him why. He told me that the autopilot causes stress and load on the airplane and it was best to hand fly. That way when the aircraft encounters turbulence you let it ride through the turbulence like a boat in the waves and then you correct the flight path by hand. If the autopilot were flying it would fight the turbulence and cause overload and overstress the airplane.

Most light airplanes produce either 14 volts or 28 volts of electricity with a belt driven alternator. On single engine airplanes you usually can see the drive belt when looking through the front of the engine cowling. Part of the preflight inspection is to determine the condition of the drive belt and its tension. While a private pilot applicant was conducting his preflight I asked him what was the purpose of the drive belt. He explained that the propeller was rotated by the engine through a system of pulleys and the drive belt. If the drive belt failed, the propeller would stop turning. I was speechless.

A candidate for CFI-ASE was explaining the electrical system of a Cessna 172-RG. He said that you could think of electrical voltage as water pressure. He continued that in order for the alternator to refill the battery the alternator would need to have a higher pressure than the battery and that is why the alternator produces 28 volts of electricity and the battery supplies 24 volts of electricity. I then asked him if there was any advantage of a 28-volt system vs. a 14-volt system. He replied that the 28-volt system used thinner wires than the 14-volt system. He finished by saying that using the water vs. voltage analogy and the Bernoulli Principle which states that when a fluid is accelerated through a restriction it increases speed, the thinner wires would cause the electricity to travel faster through the wires and the aircraft avionics and electrical systems would work faster. I thought about notifying the Nobel Prize subcommittee for physics about this scientific breakthrough.

The airspeed indicator compares the air pressure from the pilot tube with the air pressure from the static system. Movement of an internal diaphragm is amplified by mechanical means, which causes the indicator needle to move and indicate the speed of the aircraft.

Picture of an Airspeed Indicator Internal Components

An applicant for an Instrument Airplane rating explained to me that the airspeed indicator was powered by the aircraft's vacuum system. According to his theory, as the aircraft went faster through the air the vacuum pump would rotate faster and produce more vacuum. This in turn would cause the airspeed indicator needle to point to a faster indicated airspeed.

Airplane Configuration

A CFI-ASE candidate was asked to explain the purpose of the horizontal stabilizer on a Cessna 172. His explanation was that as the downwash of air from the wing hit the top of the horizontal stabilizer, that force would push down on the top of the horizontal stabilizer causing the nose of the aircraft to go up and that would balance the forces acting on the airplane. (Look in the chapter on aerodynamics to find the real purpose of the horizontal stabilizer.)

I asked him to tell me how this idea could explain a T-tail aircraft where the horizontal stabilizer is well above the downwash from the wing. He said that T-tail aircraft usually had more horsepower than conventional aircraft and the extra power kept the nose up.

Pictures of Conventional Tail and a T-tail Aircraft

Piper Aircraft designs their ailerons, flaps and elevators with indented corrugations. A popular explanation as to the purpose of the corrugations is that they help smooth out the airflow over the control surfaces. Some candidates think that the corrugations allow the air to flow faster over the control surface making it more effective. Even many CFI candidates are in the dark here. The corrugations give added strength just like in a cardboard box or an air conditioning duct. Thus Piper aircraft can use thinner material resulting in less weight and more payload for the airplane.

Picture of Piper Aileron and Flap

Cessna and Beechcraft also corrugate their control surfaces, but instead of using inward they use outward corrugations.

Picture of Cessna Aileron and Flap

General Knowledge
A basic definition of hypoxia is that it is a lack of oxygen to the brain. The atmosphere is made up of 79% nitrogen, 20% oxygen and 1% of remaining gases. The partial pressure of oxygen is 20% of the total pressure of the atmosphere. One atmosphere of pressure at sea level can be expressed as 14.7 psi, 29.92 inches of Mercury (Hg), 1012.3 millimeters of Hg or 34 feet of

water. Thus at sea level the partial pressure of oxygen would be approximately 202 millimeters. At 18,000 feet above sea level the total pressure is about 500 millimeters and the partial pressure of oxygen would be about 100 millimeters. Not enough pressure for us to get oxygen into our blood stream

We get oxygen into our blood by breathing. As we take air into our lungs oxygen is pushed through the lung membrane by its partial pressure. It takes about 140 millimeters of pressure to accomplish the push. So as we go higher and have less partial pressure of oxygen, the amount getting into our blood stream is reduced and hypoxia begins. Symptoms range from euphoria, reduction in visual acuity, loss of reasoning ability, blue colored nail and lips, drowsiness to passing out. (Sounds like a drinking spree? Same effects. The alcohol prevents oxygen from connecting to the red blood cells for transfer to the brain and remainder of your body.)

Part 91 of the Federal Air Regulations (FARs) sets forth rules about use of supplemental oxygen. Pilots of light aircraft need to know that supplemental oxygen is required by crew members for any time exceeding 30 minutes when between 12,500 feet and 14,000 feet cabin altitude. It is required by the flight crew for all time above 14,000 cabin altitude and must be available for passengers above 15,000 feet cabin altitude. The Aeronautical Information Manual (AIM) recommends that supplemental oxygen be used above 10,000 feet during the day and above 5,000 feet at night. The AIM is more conservative than the regulations.

Popular answers as to why the AIM recommends 5,000 feet at night go something like this.

At night the air is less dense so we would have trouble getting enough oxygen.

At night the air is more dense so we would take in too much oxygen causing hyperventilation.

A Private Pilot ASEL applicant said that because the night air is cooler, and thus denser, than daytime air, oxygen would settle to a lower altitude. Therefore there would be more oxygen to breath below 5,000 feet.

Another Private Pilot ASEL told me that hypoxia is caused by making an instrument approach when the weather is below landing minimums.. He further explained that due to the stress of such an approach, the pilot would most likely be afraid and would hold his breath. This would cause a deficiency of oxygen in his blood leading to hypoxia. I told him that the situation he described might cause hyperventilation, but I failed to see how it could cause hypoxia.

Takeoffs and Landings

For some people, takeoffs and landings are the most interesting part of flying. Make a smooth landing and your passengers will clap and cheer. Make a bad landing and you get booed. Students normally can make reasonable takeoffs after two instructional flights. Landings are another story. A typical student is normally approved for solo after 10 to 15 hours of instruction. During that time about half is spent learning how to land an airplane. It is an exciting time for the student and the instructor. A study several years ago found that a flight instructor teaching a student how to land an airplane has a higher heart beat rate, a higher blood pressure level, and a higher breathing rate than Neil Armstrong had when he was landing on the moon. Think about the decisions being made by the instructor. He can see a bounce coming so should he just let the student go and learn from the mistake, give some verbal coaching, or take control of the airplane. Many flight instructors have asked me when should they take control of the airplane from the student. I tell them that I mean no joke, but they will know when to take control. It is usually about the time they see their life history playing out before their eyes.

A Designated Pilot Examiner does not have the option of giving verbal coaching. The Practical Test Standards are very clear that if the Examiner has to intervene the applicant has failed the test. If we see a bounce coming we can go along for the ride, or intervene and take control of the airplane, which is an automatic failure. If there is no effort to recover from the bounce or the bounce is really bad that would also result in a failure.

During the preflight briefing I make it clear to the applicant flying a tricycle gear airplane that their landings must be on the centerline of the runway, the main wheels must touch down before the nose wheel touches down and directional control must be maintained to keep the airplane on the runway centerline during the rollout. It is disappointing that some flight instructors do such a poor job of teaching landings and enforcing the standards. I suppose it is easier to accept getting the airplane down somewhere on the pavement without any damage than demanding good performance from the student. I know that the students can do it if they try. On many check-rides the first landing is somewhere on the runway without any effort to maintain the centerline. I advise the applicant that landing on the centerline and rolling out on the centerline is as serious as a train wreck, and if landings cannot be done within the standards a pink slip will be issued. Most get the message and the remaining landings are made within standards. Flight Instructors take note. You can get good performance from your student if you demand it.

In this chapter I will give some examples of poor, bad, really bad takeoffs and landings, and fouled up approaches to landings. A few were very exciting. As every flight begins with taxi out from the parking ramp and taxi back to the parking ramp some sparkling taxi moments are also included.

Taxi Troubles

A Private Pilot ASEL applicant was preparing to taxi from the transient parking ramp at Pompano Beach Airpark (KPMP). The ground controller said, "Taxi to Runway 15 via taxiway Delta."

If you look at the airport diagram you can see all the applicant had to do was taxi out from the parking area onto Taxiway Delta and proceed northwest to Runway 15.

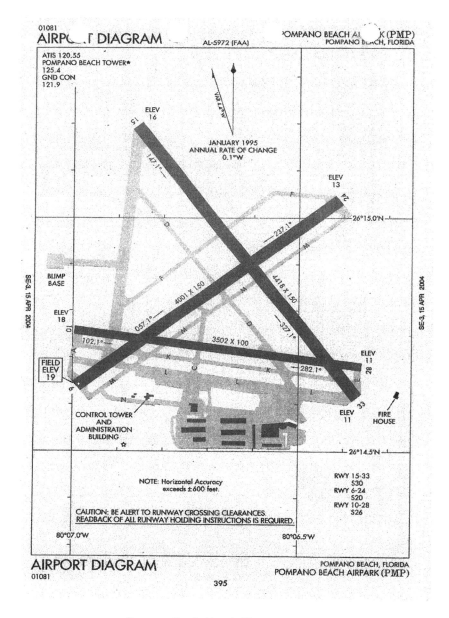

Pompano Beach Airpark Airport Diagram

Instead, the applicant turned left on Taxiway Lima and taxied west to the crossing point of Runway 6. At this point the ground controller said, "Are you taking a tour?"

The controllers at KPMP know my voice, so I called back that it was a check-ride and that we needed clearance back to the parking ramp.

The applicant looked at me and said, "Does that mean I fail?"

Same airport, different test: This time it was a CFI-ASE applicant. We were cleared to Runway 10 via Taxiway Lima. We departed the parking ramp and turned left onto Taxiway Lima. The applicant wasn't paying attention to his directional control and allowed the right main to go off the taxiway into the dirt. When I asked the applicant what he was doing, he said, "I was distracted by looking at the airport chart." He was lucky that he didn't hit a taxiway light. That would have meant a lot of paperwork. A failure caused by one of the most basic rules. Don't move the airplane unless you are looking outside.

During another check-ride at KPMP an applicant for Commercial Pilot ASEL was told to hold short of Runway 6. The applicant read back the clearance, "Hold short of Runway 6." Then he started to taxi out onto Runway 6. I retarded the throttle to idle and stepped on the brakes. Too late. We had crossed the hold short line onto the active runway without a clearance. I asked him, "What were you thinking?"

He replied, "I got confused." Lucky for him it was a check-ride and the tower was in a forgiving mood.

A Private Pilot ASEL applicant was preparing to taxi from the parking ramp at North County Airport (F45). He listened to the automated weather observation service (AWOS) that was advising that the prevailing wind was from 080 degrees at a speed of seven knots. As there is no tower at this airport the pilot has to make his own decisions about what runway to use. The reported wind made it obvious that the runway of choice should be Runway 8R. Runway 8L is a grass runway and is mostly used for helicopter training.

North County Airport (F45)

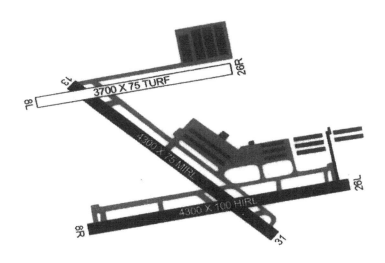

FREQUENCIES

F45 CTAF	123.075
F45 Unicom	131.25
F45 AWOS	119.975
PBI Clnc Del (F45 On Ground)	120.82
Gwinn Tower	120.4
PBI App/Dep (N)	124.6
PBI App/Dep (S)	125.2
PBI App/Dep	128.25
Miami Center	132.25
Miami FSS	122.4
Miami FSS (PHK vicinity)	122.35
Miami FSS (FPR vicinity)	122.55

TELEPHONE NUMBERS

FSS	1-800-922-7433
SunQuest	(561) 627-0037
Landmark (F45)	(561) 626-9799
F45 AWOS	(561) 630-6932
PBI ATIS	(561) 689-2847
PBI Customs	(561) 233-1080

IFR Clearances

PBI ATC	(561) 683-1867
PBI ATC (after 6pm)	(561) 684-2446
PBI Tower	(561) 478-4456

Airport Diagram for North County Airport

The applicant taxied out of the parking ramp onto Taxiway F and headed toward Runway 8R. As we taxied out he passed a windsock that indicated the wind was from the east. When we arrived at Runway 8R he stopped the airplane because another airplane was taking off from Runway 8R. It passed in front of us from right to left. After it passed the applicant continued his taxi to the end of Taxiway F and proceeded to complete his before takeoff checks. Then he taxied onto Runway 31 and started his takeoff. I told him to abort the takeoff and stop short of Runway 8R. Then I asked him, "Did you listen to the AWOS?"

He replied, "Yes."

Then I asked him, "Did you see the windsock as we taxied out?"

He replied, "Yes."

I continued the questioning with, "Did you see the airplane that took off in front of us?"

He replied, "Yes."

I asked the final question, "Then why are you taking off on Runway 31?"

His answer was, "Duh, because I used it last time I flew with my instructor."

That was one of the shortest check-rides I have ever done.

An applicant completed the flight portion of his Private Pilot ASEL check-ride with a landing on Runway 8R at F45 and exited onto the parallel taxiway. I advised him to taxi to parking. When he reached the intersection with Runway 31 instead of crossing over to Taxiway F and then to the ramp he turned left onto Runway 31. I asked him why he was taxiing on a runway. He said, "I made a mistake."

Check-rides in Piper Aztecs (PA-23) have a built-in excitement factor. Some of the older Aztecs only have brakes on the pilot side. I have to be very alert when conducting a check-ride in these aircraft as I don't have any ability to brake the aircraft myself. During a Commercial Pilot AMEL check-ride we had landed at Boca Raton airport (KBCT). After exiting the runway the controller cleared us to taxi to and hold short of Runway 23. The applicant repeated the instruction to, "Hold short of Runway 23."

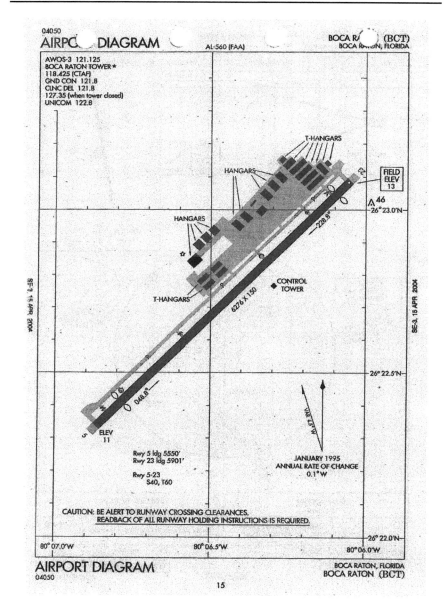

Boca Raton Airport Diagram

As we reached the end of the taxiway it became apparent that the applicant was not going to stop at the hold short line for Runway 23. I observed a Lear Jet on base leg for Runway 23 and estimated that we both would arrive on the end of Runway 23 at the same time. I said to the applicant, "Stop the airplane." There was no response as we made the turn from the taxiway to the Runway 23 entrance, I said in a really loud voice, "Stop the airplane." Still no response. We started to cross the hold short line and I saw the Lear Jet turn from base to final. I whacked the applicant on his shoulder to get his attention and yelled as loud as I could, "Stop the airplane!!" He finally stopped the Aztec on the numbers of Runway 23. The Lear Jet had passed just in front of us and had landed on Runway 23. The Boca Tower controller was apoplectic. I told the tower controller that this was a check-ride, that there were no brakes on my side of the airplane and that I had been repeatedly trying to get the applicant to stop short of Runway 23.

The controller asked, "How is the check-ride going?"

I replied, "There is a pink slip in the applicant's immediate future." That seemed to calm the tower controller and he cleared us for takeoff. After we returned to our departure airport (FXE), I asked the applicant what was he thinking at Boca Raton? He said he had become preoccupied with the Before Takeoff Checklist and forgot that we were supposed to hold short.

A favorite way to end a check-ride isn't limited to students trying to obtain their Private Pilot certificate. An Airline Transport Pilot AMEL candidate completed his Before Taxi checklist and advanced the throttles to begin taxi. The airplane didn't move. He checked that the parking brake was released and tried again. Still the airplane didn't move. He said that he thought the airplane had settled into the blacktop that had been softened by the heat of the sun. He advanced the throttles to full open and the airplane still didn't move. Then I suggested that he stop the engines and go outside to investigate. It didn't take too long for him to discover that he had forgotten to remove the wheel chocks. What ever happened to a final walk around before getting into the airplane?

A Commercial Pilot AMEL was performing his Before Takeoff Checks in a Beechcraft Baron 55 (BE-55). The Baron has an electric fuel boost pump for each engine. The pump can be in OFF, LOW or HIGH. The LOW position is used to prevent vapor locks when the ambient temperature is high. The HIGH position is used to prime the engine for starting. It may not be used for takeoff because the engine may become flooded. The Examiner cannot readily see the control switch position due to its location on the pilot side of the control panel. This applicant mistakenly selected the HIGH position during the run up. When he reduced the power to idle both engines stopped due to flooding. He just sat there dumbfounded as to why the engines had stopped. I leaned way over so I could see the auxiliary pump control switches and determine what he might have done. I asked him why he had selected the HIGH position. He said, "The fuel tanks are only three quarter full and I didn't want to suck any air into the engines."

Takeoff Follies

A CFI-AME applicant demonstrated a short field landing and then taxied back to the runway for a takeoff. He called the tower for takeoff clearance.

Before the aircraft moved I asked him, "Did you complete the Before Takeoff Checklist?"

He said, "Yes I did." As he taxied out onto the runway I called the tower and cancelled our takeoff.

I said to the applicant, "I guess you missed the part of the checklist that has you check the flap setting." He had never retracted the flaps from the Full Down landing position to the Full Up takeoff position. He would have attempted a takeoff with the flaps in their Full Down position. He had done the After Landing Checklist and the Before Takeoff Checklist like a robot. He was just reading them without checking anything. During his debrief I told him about two major airline crashes caused by taking off with the incorrect flap setting.

A Commercial Pilot ASEL applicant was beginning the flight portion of his check-ride in a Cessna 172-RG with a soft field takeoff. For non-pilots, this maneuver simulates taking off from a grass airport or a runway fouled with mud or snow. The idea is to rotate the aircraft at a slower than normal takeoff speed and keep the aircraft just above the runway in ground effect until a normal climb speed is attained. The applicant had his left foot too high on the left pedal and was inadvertently applying pressure to the left brake. For non-pilots, most airplane brake systems are designed so pilots can apply differential brake pressure to each wheel. Part of pilot training is to learn how to apply equal brake pressure with each foot. Because the applicant was applying pressure to the left brake the airplane was lurching along during the takeoff roll. When it became airborne the airplane rapidly accelerated. The applicant misjudged how high to fly the airplane in ground effect and allowed it to descend back onto the runway with his left foot still actuating the left brake.. When the airplane contacted the runway it veered sharply to the left heading for the grass between the runway and the parallel taxiway. As the airplane skidded nose left the right wing lifted into the air and it looked like the left wing tip would strike the ground. I had to takeover control of the aircraft. The airplane was beginning to rollover into the grass when I was finally able to overpower his left foot. I used the entire 3000-foot length of the runway to recover and bring the airplane to a stop. After a few seconds of silence the tower controller said, "I presume that you will be returning to the ramp?"

Another Commercial Pilot ASEL candidate was performing a takeoff in a Cessna 172-RG. The airspeed indicator was showing 50 knots and the wheels were still on the ground. The applicant reached out and moved the landing gear handle to the UP position. As I heard the landing gear hydraulic motor begin to run I grabbed the control yoke and yanked the airplane up into ground effect. I was very afraid that when the landing gear retracted the main gear would strike the runway as the Cessna 172-RG landing gear drops down before it retracts to the rear. Lucky me, I was high enough that the landing gear did not strike the runway. When I asked the applicant what he was thinking, he said, "I was trying to adjust the carburetor heat knob."

A CFI-ASE applicant set the parking brake on a Piper Arrow prior to engine start. The applicant completed the After Start and Before Taxi checklists and began to taxi to the run up area but forgot to release the parking brake. During the taxi I said, "It seems that you are using a lot of power to taxi"

She said, "The airplane is very heavy today and it will take a lot of power." The Before Takeoff checklist was completed and we taxied out onto the runway but the applicant still hadn't released the parking brake. With full power the airplane barely accelerated to about 15 knots. We continued along for about 200 feet to where I couldn't take anymore. I pointed out the position of the parking brake handle and said to release it and taxi back to the ramp. Then she said, "Does that mean I fail?"

A Commercial Pilot AMEL candidate performed a takeoff from KFXE in a Diamond Twinstar (DA-42). As we climbed out through 2000 feet he entered a cloud. I said to him, "I don't recall getting an IFR clearance."

He said, "You're right. We shouldn't be in the cloud." Then he suddenly pulled back on the stick raising the nose of the aircraft so high that the aircraft exceeded the critical angle of attack and stalled. He was oblivious to his rudder position. (Just as in a single engine airplane the DA-42 has P factor during climb and you must hold right rudder pressure.) So the ball was out on the right side and the aircraft broke to the left. I took over the aircraft and regained control after about 90 degrees of turn and flew us back to the airport. During the debrief the applicant said he had pulled up on the stick because he thought we could come out of the cloud top into clear weather.

It's this kind of ride that makes me wonder, "Why am I doing this?"

Sometimes the airport layout confuses pilots. At North Perry Airport (KHWO) airplanes that are parked on the south side are usually cleared to taxi to Runway 9R via Taxiway Lima when there is an easterly wind. The Before Takeoff Checklist is accomplished on Taxiway Bravo and then the pilot calls for takeoff clearance. The normal procedure is to continue to taxi west on Taxiway Lima to Runway 36L, turn north on Runway 36L and make a right turn onto Runway 9R.

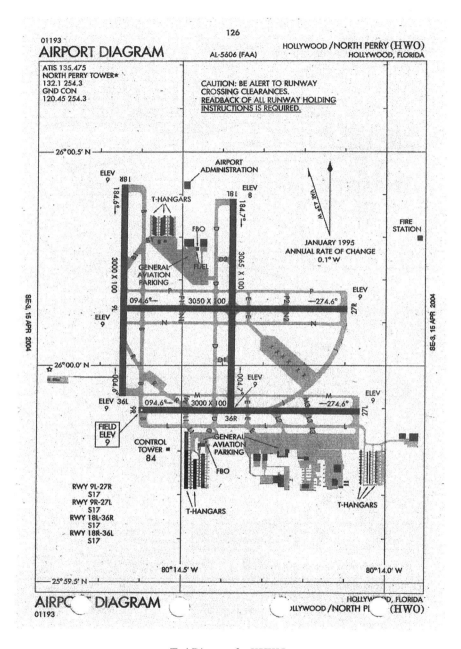

Taxi Diagram for KHWO

A Private Pilot ASEL applicant finished his before takeoff checks and called for takeoff clearance. The tower cleared him for takeoff on Runway 9R.

The applicant turned onto Runway 36L and advanced the throttle to takeoff power. As we accelerated past Runway 9R I closed the throttle and asked the tower for clearance back to parking. The applicant said he thought he was on Runway 9R not Runway 36L. He never thought to check that his magnetic compass heading was in agreement with the runway heading.

Landings and Angst

Almost nothing compares to the feeling of making a really good landing. The kind where the wheels just start rolling and you can't feel the airplane contact the ground. That is the pilot's goal. The Practical Test Standards set forth requirements for landings such as how accurately the airplane must be flown to the touchdown point including speed and direction control and control of the aircraft's path during the rollout. In this section I have highlighted short field, soft field, and crosswind landings, forward slips to landing, approaching the airport for landing I and have finished with some really bad landings.

Short Field Landings
Short field landings are used when the runway is short and/or there is an obstacle in the approach path to the runway. A good rule of thumb to calculate the required runway length is the 60% rule. If the computed landing distance is 1800 feet, then a safe runway length would be 3000 feet.

$$0.6x = 1800$$
$$x = 3000$$

You would not be in violation of any Federal Air Regulation landing on a runway 1800 feet long if that was your calculated landing distance, but you might not be the brightest bulb in the string of Christmas lights. It's always best to be conservative. Remember that the data used to develop the performance charts in the Operating Handbook is based on flight tests using a new airplane flown by a factory test pilot. The book number is best you could ever do.

The PVT-ASEL applicant attempted a short field landing in a C-172. The aircraft manual recommends that the approach be flown with full flaps at 63 knots. This applicant decided to make the approach at 85 knots. Arriving over the runway too high and too fast he pushed forward on the yoke in an attempt to land on the numbers. He landed on the nose wheel and after 3 bounces, each one becoming more exciting, I had to take control of the aircraft.

The COM-ASEL applicant attempted a short field landing over an obstacle in a C-172RG. The approach was flown at +/- 65 knots with full flaps but the approach path was incorrect. The applicant, "dragged," the aircraft at nearly full power for the last mile at 100 AGL and when he passed the imaginary 50-foot tree, he reduced power to idle and made a very steep drop to a hard landing on the runway. When I asked him what the FAA Flight

Training Handbook showed for a short field landing descent path, he said, "I haven't read that book." What? How can you be ready for a flight test if you haven't read the book? You would be amazed at the number of applicants who admit to not having read the FAA Flight Training Handbook.

The COM-AMEL applicant attempted a short field landing over an obstacle in a PA-44. The aircraft performance charts indicated a final approach speed of 70 knots with full flaps for our landing weight. The applicant flew the approach at 90 knots using a flap setting of 25 degrees until over the runway threshold when he closed the throttles and set full flaps touching down 500 feet past the intended landing point. When I asked the applicant why the approach had been flown at such a fast speed with partial flaps, he said that he had kept the speed above single engine climb speed (88 knots) until landing had been assured. Then I pointed out to him that the Pilot's Operating Handbook for the airplane recommended a final approach speed of 70 knots for our landing weight with flaps at full down position and that if he had flown according to the book he would have been able to land within the Practical Test Standard limit of 100 feet past the intended point of landing. His reply was, "The book is wrong. My way is much safer." Amazing, isn't it? This pilot knows more than the Piper Aircraft engineers about how to fly the PA-44.

The CFI-ASE applicant was demonstrating and teaching a short field landing in a C-172RG. The approach was flown at 90 knots vs. the recommended 63 knots and the aircraft was too high and too fast on short final. So the applicant put the aircraft into a steep slip to lose the altitude and the aircraft arrived over the threshold at a speed of 100 knots and touched down 1000 feet past the point of intended landing. When I asked about the placard that said, "Avoid slips with flaps extended," he replied that the placard was, "only advisory," and could be disregarded when a slip was, "necessary to make the runway."

Many check ride failures are due to a poorly executed short field approach to landing. It always starts with poor instruction. I have asked many applicants how the procedure is described in the FAA Flight Training Handbook and watch applicant shoulders shrug and see an embarrassed look as they admit they have no idea what is in the book because they haven't read it. Egads! What are you CFIs doing? How can you properly teach any maneuver without reviewing the recommended procedures with your student?

Soft Field Landings

When I learned to fly we were taught that a soft field landing was the reverse of a soft field takeoff. In the Cessna training aircraft we used 10 degrees of flaps and in the Piper Cherokees we used two notches of flaps. We approached at the normal recommended speed and as we flared the aircraft we added one or two hundred rpm above idle to the power. In constant speed propeller aircraft we added one or two inches of manifold pressure above idle. This added power kept the aircraft floating in ground effect as we slowly increased back pressure until the main wheels made a soft touchdown. We held backpressure to keep the nose gear from touching down as long as we could.

Our instructors had us try to hold the nose wheel about six inches above the runway as long as possible until the nose settled to the runway.

Now the applicants use full flaps. Maybe this change is the result of interpreting the FAA recommendation that on landings maximum flap setting for conditions should be used. You can still make very soft landings with full flaps if you make the slight power adjustment during the flare. This is where the modern applicants have their problem. They omit the slight power increase and end up making a normal landing that frequently is not even close to a soft touchdown. Another problem is applicants add too much power in the flare and float forever. Many times this will result in a bounced landing or loss of directional control due to a crosswind component.

A Private Pilot ASEL was performing a soft field landing in a Cessna 172 and kept the power setting one or two hundred rpm above idle during the flare. It looked like it was going to work out. The problem was that I couldn't see from my side of the airplane that he had his feet too high on the pedals and had the brakes on when we touched down. When the main wheels touched the pavement the sudden lurch slammed the nose wheel down onto the runway and the airplane went up onto the nose wheel and the main wheels went up into the air. We call this wheel barrowing. Then the main wheels slammed onto the runway and the nose wheel went back into the air. We merrily continued bouncing down the runway like this with the applicant yelling, "Please help me," until I could get control and stop the airplane. The applicant's explanation for all of this was, "I must have had the parking brake set by accident."

Crosswind Landings

Private, Commercial, ATP and CFI applicants all have trouble with crosswind landings. It starts with poor primary instruction. I see flight schools increasingly restricting student flying when there is a strong crosswind. When is a better time to practice? Or is it that many Flight Instructors can't handle a crosswind?

There are two ways to make an approach in a crosswind. The crab method and the wing low method. I personally prefer the crab method but either is acceptable.

To properly fly the crab method you fly down the runway extended centerline crabbing into the wind keeping the wings level. Just as you enter the flare you lower the upwind wing with aileron movement and use opposite rudder to align the aircraft's longitudinal axis with the runway centerline. Touchdown is made on the upwind main wheel, then the opposite main wheel is lowered to the runway followed by lowering the nose wheel. Increasing aileron deflection into the wind is needed to help maintain the aircraft on the runway centerline. This method works well with aircraft having wing mounted engines.

The wing low method is a modified forward slip to landing. The ailerons are used to lower the upwind wing sufficiently to hold the extended runway centerline. Opposite rudder is used to align to aircraft's longitudinal axis with the runway centerline. Touchdown and rollout control movements are the same as with the crab method. This method will alert you early during the approach that the crosswind is exceeding aileron and rudder ability to maintain the runway centerline.

When I was instructing I made sure the student could fly both methods and then let the student pick which he liked best. Most pilots subconsciously combine the two methods during their crosswind landings.

What goes wrong on the flight tests? Or rather, what doesn't go wrong?

Unable to maintain runway extended centerline during descent

Touch down with aircraft's longitudinal axis not aligned with runway centerline.

Unable to maintain directional control after touch down

The second mistake leads to some exciting rollouts. I remember a CFI-ASE applicant who relaxed the flight controls during the flare. The airplane began to weathervane into the wind and touched down with a side drift on the downwind main wheel. Immediately after touchdown the aircraft began careening towards the edge of the runway. It was completely out of the applicant's control I had to take over the aircraft. During the debrief I asked the applicant why he had relaxed the ailerons during the flare. He said, "We were on the ground and the flight controls wouldn't work very good, so I had to steer with the nose wheel." A complete lack of understanding how to do a crosswind landing.

Forward Slips to Landing

I have always been amazed at the uniformly bad forward slip to landing techniques demonstrated by Private and CFI applicants Many of the Private applicants give me the usual, "My instructor never showed me this," (Ha-Ha-Ha). They are dumfounded when I remind them that a forward slip is a maneuver required to be learned before first solo.

Most of the bad forward slips to landing are caused by excessive speed on final approach. The typical Cessna single engine aircraft used for training, the 152, 172 and 172RG, recommend a landing speed with no flaps of approximately 60–70 knots. The applicants like to slip at 90 knots. When I ask them why they are going so fast, a popular answer is, "So I don't stall." This shows a lack of understanding aerodynamics. Recommended approach speed is 1.3 times the stall speed, which is around 45 knots with no flaps for the typical training aircraft so 60–65 knots on approach is just about right.

Another poor technique is to begin the slip so far out that you have to level off and add power to make the runway. The maneuver should be flown so that the aircraft slips to a point just past the end of the runway at flare altitude and is then straightened out and flared to land. There is a placard in most of the Cessna 172 and 172 RG aircraft that reads, "Avoid slips with flaps extended." You would be amazed at the number of pilots who do not see the placard or disregard the warning. At the risk of getting a lot of hate mail, I will give the short reason for the placard. When in a slip with flaps extended, airflow over the elevator and rudder surfaces is disturbed and they will lose their effectiveness. Some of the older Cessna manuals state that the elevator may oscillate during a slip with flaps extended under certain combinations of density altitude, aircraft weight and center of gravity location. Will the airplane crash if you slip with flaps? I don't know of anyone who has crashed slipping with flaps extended, but CFI applicants get no slack about this. If they try to teach me to slip with flaps extended in an aircraft placarded to avoid such maneuvers, they fail. One CFI-ASE candidate wanted to debate the meaning of, "Avoid." In his mind that meant it was optional. If a pilot wanted to slip with flaps extended it was his call. The word, "Avoid," was not a limitation. And this applicant was a native English speaker.

I recall a Private applicant who was doing a slip to landing on a 4400-foot runway. Happily slipping at 90 knots in a Cessna 152, over the end of the runway at 150 feet and beginning his flare 2000 feet down the runway. Due to the high speed and action by ground effect, we still hadn't touched down after 3500 feet of runway. He had it in his mind that we were going to land and started to push the nose forward. I took over control and began a go-around. He looked like a deer in the headlights when I asked him if he hadn't seen the end of the runway approaching and realized that we were going too fast to stop. He was mind locked so deep into making the landing that he lost his situational awareness.

Really Bad Landings

I have been shown some really bad landings by a variety of applicants. Some of the more memorable are described below.

A COM-ASEL applicant was demonstrating a short field landing in gusty conditions. The gust factor was 15 knots. He allowed the airspeed to get too low and when the wind slowed 15 knots the airplane fell to the runway from about 10 feet hitting tail first due to the high angle of attack as he tried to cushion the landing by pulling back on the control yoke. During the after landing inspection I noticed that the tail tie down hook had been knocked off so I wrote up the maintenance discrepancy as, "Tail tie down hook shows signs of excessive wear." The mechanics and I had a good laugh about that. The applicant claimed that his instructor had never told him about adding half the gust factor to the landing reference speed.

A CFI-AME applicant was demonstrating a short field landing in a BE-76 and for some unknown reason forgot to flare the airplane. We hit very hard. We hit so hard that my legs and feet were numb. I told the applicant to taxi to the FBO and that I had numbness in my legs and feet most likely caused by compression of my spine and if I were still numb when we arrived at the FBO we would be calling the paramedics. By the time we reached the FBO feeling had returned to my legs and feet. An inspection by a mechanic revealed that the right main landing gear attachment had been bent and repairs were needed. This applicant provided the title for this book when he then asked me, "Does that mean I fail?"

An Instrument Airplane applicant was completing a circling approach. Just after touchdown the airplane veered sharply to the right heading for the grass between the runway and the taxiway. The applicant screamed that something was wrong and she couldn't control the airplane. I had to take control of the airplane. I gave it full power, pulled back on the yoke to get airborne before going into the depression between the runway and the taxiway and pushed hard on the rudder pedals to align the aircraft with its direction of flight. As she screamed in pain I realized what had been the trouble. She had been wearing high platform shoes and had somehow gotten one of her feet caught under a rudder pedal hindering pedal travel.

You would expect that an applicant for Airline Transport Pilot (ATP) AMEL would be able to land an airplane without incident. Never take anything for granted on a check-ride. This applicant landed a Piper Seminole (PA-44) with his feet high up on the pedals, which activated the brakes. We touched down with full brakes and the airplane began lurching, skidding and swerving towards the edge of the runway. I started to see my life story roll past my eyes so I took control of the airplane. I had to use all my leg power to regain steering. The applicant was moaning in pain. Then I saw what was causing the trouble. He was wearing cowboy boots and because of the high heels had somehow tangled one of his feet under one of the rudder pedals and I was crushing his foot as I pushed on my pedals.

The other footwear extreme is the open toe sandal. I call them Bible shoes. You know the shoe. All of your toes are waving in the air. The sole is fastened to your foot with one or two straps. You might as well fly barefoot. An applicant appeared in a pair of these and I told him to go home and get a real pair of shoes to fly with. He wasn't too happy with me at first but quickly discovered why I wouldn't fly with him in the sandals as he walked out of the room and smashed his unprotected little toe into the door jam. Fortunately he didn't break it and we were able to conduct the flight test later that day.

Flight 54 Where Are You?

Before you can land on the runway you have to find it. This is called making an approach to the airport. Here are some approaches that are truly eye rolling.

A Commercial Pilot ASEL applicant was approaching Pompano Beach Airpark (KPMP) from the northwest. There was a strong wind from the northeast and the tower controller said to enter a left base for Runway 6. For non-pilots this would be a path that would put us at a 90 degree angle to Runway 6. I watched as the applicant continued inbound and I finally said, "It looks like you're lining up with Runway 10."

The applicant said, "It looks that way because I'm crabbing for wind." The applicant let the northeast wind drift us over to the extended centerline of Taxiway Lima, which parallels Runway 10 and he continued inbound. At 200 feet above the ground I called the tower and announced a go-around.

I asked, "Didn't you see the airplanes parked at the edge of the taxiway?"

He said, "The water on the pavement and the sun glare confused me. I've never landed on wet pavement before."

A Private Pilot ASEL test was concluding with a landing at Pompano Beach Airpark. We were approaching from the northwest and the wind was from the northwest. We were slightly west of the airport so the tower directed us to, "Report midfield left downwind for Runway 33." For non-pilots the tower wanted us to fly parallel to Runway 33 on the west side of the airport and call the tower at the midfield point. The applicant instead maneuvered for a right downwind on the east side of the airport and crossed over the extended centerline of Runway 33. I saw a Piper Twin Comanche (PA-24) taking off from Runway 33 and called the tower. I said we were on a check-ride, I saw the airplane taking off and could the tower give me some leeway. At the midfield point on the right downwind I asked the applicant if anything might be amiss.

He said, "Oh, I'm on the wrong side." I asked him if he had seen the airplane taking off from Runway 33 and that he had passed very close to it. He said that he had not seen the other airplane.

Another Private Pilot ASEL was approaching KPMP from the north along the coastline. The tower told him to report passing the lighthouse and to expect Runway 33. The Hillsboro Inlet Lighthouse is a 100-year-old treasure that was restored a few years ago. The beacon can be seen 20 miles out to sea. It is a great landmark used by Pompano Tower to help control the flow of traffic in their airspace. The applicant did not report passing the lighthouse and started to enter a right base for Runway 33. He did not see another airplane on left base for Runway 33 and continued on a head-on collision course. I had to take over the airplane to avoid disaster. I called the tower and advised we were on a check-ride and requested to make a 360-degree left turn to re-enter a right base for Runway 33 and a full stop landing. The tower said, "Is a pink slip in the future?"

The applicant said, "What did I do?" During the debrief after landing the applicant said that he had become so focused on making a good landing that he had forgotten the instruction to report passing the lighthouse.

A Commercial Pilot ASEL applicant was cleared to land on Runway 28 by Pompano Tower. The applicant lined up on Runway 24. When we were close to the airport I asked the applicant what number was on the runway. He said he had lined up on the wrong runway. I asked him how did that happen. He said, "The wind blew me and I haven't been to this airport before."

A Private Pilot ASEL departed Pompano Beach Airpark for Ft. Lauderdale Executive Airport (KFXE). Overhead the Pompano Beach City Fishing Pier, Executive Tower was contacted for landing clearance. The tower advised to report on a left downwind for Runway 8. About one mile east of KFXE the applicant reduced power, set 10 degrees of flaps and began to descend from the pattern altitude of 1000 feet. At 700 feet I noticed that his eyes were focused on the approach end of Runway 26. When I asked him why we were at 700 feet he said, "I don't know."

I told him, "Climb back to 1000 feet."

Shortly thereafter, the tower said, "Extend downwind, I will call your base." At that point we were opposite the approach end of Runway 13. The applicant immediately began to descend on a base leg for Runway 13. I had to take over the airplane so we didn't interfere with other traffic.

During the debrief I asked, "What were you thinking?"

He replied, "I was confused."

A Commercial Pilot ASEL was approaching Pahokee Airport (KPHK) from the southeast. Listening to the Unicom frequency indicated that Runway 35 was in use. He said that he planned to overfly the airport at 1500 feet and enter a left downwind to Runway 35. He flew over the airport and descended to pattern altitude of 1000 feet and reported on left downwind for Runway 35. The problem was that he was flying a right downwind for Runway 17. Luckily there was no other traffic in the pattern at that time. When we turned to final I asked him what was the number on the runway in front of us. He said, "Uh-oh. I think I made a mistake."

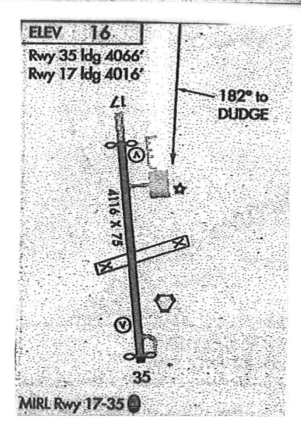

PAHOKEE/PALM BEACH COUNTY GLADES (PHK)

ELEV 16
Rwy 35 ldg 4066'
Rwy 17 ldg 4016'

182° to DUDGE

4116 X 75

MIRL Rwy 17-35

A Private Pilot ASEL was asked to proceed to Opa-Locka Airport (KOPF) for a landing. The student saw Miami International Airport (KMIA) and mistook it for KOPA. In his defense the two airports look similar when approaching from the northwest but a pilot should not mistake one for the other. As the applicant was about to enter Class B Airspace around KMIA, I had to intervene and direct a 180-degree turn. The applicant said "I thought I was on course for Opa-Locka."

Almost Landings

An applicant for Commercial Pilot AMEL became so focused on making a simulated engine out landing in a Piper Seminole (PA-44) that he forgot to extend the landing gear opposite his touchdown point while on the downwind leg. He didn't check the landing gear position on base leg and he didn't check it on final. He was so focused that he didn't hear the landing gear warning horn. On short final at 300 above the ground the tower called and said, "It doesn't appear that your gear is down." I thanked the tower and said that it was a check-ride and that I had planned to intervene at 200 feet above the ground.

The applicant said the usual, "Does that mean I fail?" During the debrief I told the applicant that he had lots of company. Two weeks earlier a CFI-AME had done the same thing during a simulated engine out landing demonstration.

A Commercial Pilot ASEL was performing a 180-degree accuracy landing in a Piper Arrow (PA-28-201R). For non-pilots this maneuver is performed by extending the landing gear on the downwind leg and reducing the power to idle opposite the touchdown point. The idea is to glide the airplane to a landing not before and not more than 200 feet past the intended point of landing. This applicant misjudged his descent profile and was heading for a landing in the grass about 25 feet short of the runway. At 50 feet above the ground with the stall warning blaring, I said to the applicant that he should think about a go-around. There was no response so I took over and landed the airplane. When I asked the applicant what he was thinking he said, "I thought I could stretch it to the runway." He had become so intent on landing on his spot that he forgot about flying the airplane.

A Private Pilot ASEL applicant was flying a traffic pattern in preparation for landing. In every left turn the coordination ball was deflected full right. As we turned from base leg to final the ball was deflected full right and the applicant allowed the airspeed to become too slow. The airplane began to exhibit a stall buffet at which time I took control and landed the airplane. During the debrief the applicant said, "The ball was on the right because I was pushing the left rudder to make the airplane turn."

Well, enough about takeoffs and landings. There are other fish to fry.

Instrument Flight Rules

The Instrument Airplane and Certified Flight Instructor-Instrument Airplane (CFI-IA) applicants have a first attempt failure rate of approximately 50%. In addition to handling the aircraft, the applicant must have substantial knowledge of instrument flight rules, ATC procedures and must be able to interpret various charts.

What is really distressing to an examiner is when, during the oral portion of the practical test, it becomes obvious that the applicant has not read the materials and has no understanding of how to apply the information contained in them. I stop the test and advise the applicant that they have not met the standard required. I then offer to review what materials that should be studied before coming back for the retest. This review usually takes about one hour.

CFIs take note. Make sure your instrument applicants have read and understand applicable sections of Part 61 and Part 91; Aim Chapter One, reference GPS; Aim Chapter Five, ATC Procedures; Aim Chapter Six, reference loss of communications procedures; and Aim Chapter Seven, reference altimeter setting procedures. In addition, review various approach plates, departure and arrival procedures, and en route charts so your applicant can easily interpret unfamiliar navigation charts. It's a good idea for your student to purchase or download from the FAA website the Instrument Rating Practical Test Standard and review its contents. The FAA also has two great books that are must-reads for your applicants: Instrument Flying Handbook and Instrument Procedures.

Picture of Instrument Flying Handbook

Instrument Procedures

U.S. Department
of Transportation
**Federal Aviation
Administration**

FAA-S-8081-4E
Effective January 2010
With Changes 1 and 2—03/16/10

Instrument Rating
For Airplane, Helicopter and Powered Lift

Practical Test Standards

Flight Standards Service
Washington, DC 20591

Reprinted by Aviation Supplies & Academics, Inc.
Newcastle, Washington

Picture of Instrument PTS

Part 61 Instrument Rating Requirements

Very distressing is the performance of CFI-IA candidates when asked to detail the Part 61 requirements that must be met by their students in order to be eligible for the Instrument Airplane practical test. Most can recite that the applicant needs 40 hours of instrument experience and that 15 of those hours must be logged as dual instruction from an, "Instrument Instructor." Now it gets interesting. About one third of the CFI applicants do not know that 20 of the 40 hours must be **in an aircraft** and only 20 hours in a simulator or flight training device (FTD) can be credited toward the 40 hour total unless the training is done under Part 142 in which case the creditable amount is 30 hours. Three fourths of the CFI applicants do not know the difference between a simulator and a FTD (a simulator has motion). This lack of knowledge leads to incorrectly filling out the flight experience section of FAA Form 8710 (the test application), which means a correction if done by ACRA or a new application if done by IACRA.

Almost none of the CFI applicants are aware of Advisory Circular 61-126 that provides information regarding the use of and crediting time obtained from a Personal Computer Based Aviation Training Device (PCATD). Under strict rules set out in the Advisory Circular, 10 hours of PCATD instruction may be credited toward the 40 hour requirement. Read AC61-126. Playing B-747 captain on your Microsoft flight simulator doesn't count.

**U.S. Department
of Transportation**

**Federal Aviation
Administration**

Advisory
Circular

Subject: QUALIFICATION AND APPROVAL OF PERSONAL COMPUTER-BASED AVIATION TRAINING DEVICES	Date: 5/12/97 Initiated By: AFS-840	AC No: 61-126 Change:

1. PURPOSE. This Advisory Circular (AC) provides information and guidance to potential training device manufacturers and aviation training consumers concerning a means, acceptable to the Administrator, by which personal computer-based aviation training devices (PCATD) may be qualified and approved for flight training toward satisfying the instrument rating training under the provisions of Title 14 of the Code of Federal Regulations (14 CFR) parts 61 and 141. While these guidelines are not mandatory, they are derived from extensive Federal Aviation Administration (FAA) and industry experience in determining compliance with the pertinent parts of 14 CFR. Mandatory terms used in this AC such as "shall" and "must" are used only in the sense of ensuring applicability of this method of compliance. PCATD's are distinct from flight training devices (FTD) qualified under AC 120-45, Airplane Flight Training Device Qualification, and flight simulators qualified under AC 120-40, Airplane Simulator Qualification. It also provides acceptable criteria under which the airplane or FTD flight-hour training time required for an instrument rating may be reduced by using PCATD's that have been determined to meet acceptable FAA standards. This AC details only one means of determining the acceptability of such devices for use in instrument training curricula.

2. RELATED 14 CFR SECTIONS. Sections of the regulations related to the information in this AC are in parts 61 and 141.

3. DEFINITIONS.

    a. PCATD. A device which:

        (1) Meets or exceeds the criteria shown in Appendix 1.

        (2) Functionally provides a training platform for at least the procedural aspects of flight relating to an instrument training curriculum.

        (3) Has been qualified by the FAA.

    b. Qualification Guide. Design criteria to assist in the evaluation and qualification process for PCATD's. A Qualification Guide is included in Appendix 1.

Picture of AC61-126

Half of the CFI applicants cannot correctly explain the long cross-country requirements for the instrument rating. Most can recite that the trip must be at least 250 nm with three different approaches being flown but they miss the part that the approaches must use navigation systems, not flown as radar approaches. So once in awhile I have an applicant that must repeat the long instrument cross-county. Another small detail about the trip is not understood by most of the CFI applicants. The trip could be accomplished using only two airports if two approaches were flown at one airport and one approach flown at the other, but a landing must be made at the distant airport or the trip does not qualify as a cross-country flight. See Part 61.1, (b), (3), (i) (A) and (ii), (B). Only military pilots are relieved of the landing requirement. See Part 61.1, (b), (3), (v), (B). A prudent CFI will do at least a touch and go at the distant airports to avoid the risk of their applicant repeating the long cross-country.

The applicant needs 50 hours cross country experience as Pilot in Command (PIC). When an examiner sees 50.0 on the application, the logbook has to be closely reviewed page by page and the time verified. You would be amazed how many times an arithmetic error is discovered and the applicant is short one or two hours. Why can't the CFI-IA see this before he arranges the flight test? The short answer is they take the word of the applicant that the requirements are met and do not check it themselves.

You would think that the basic information set forth above, the bread and butter of getting a student qualified as to the instrument rating experience requirements, would be easily explained by the CFI candidates. I just shake my head in amazement.

Part 91 Instrument Flight Rules

FAR Part 91.167 through 91.193 contains the instrument flight rules that must be understood and applied by instrument pilots. I will go through them one by one.

91.167 sets forth fuel requirements for flight in IFR conditions. Most applicants have no trouble with this rule.

91.169 sets out information required on IFR flight plans. When I ask when an alternate airport is required most applicants recite the 1-2-3 rule. Plus or minus one hour of ETA the weather must be ceiling at least 2000 feet and at least 3sm visibility. Careful reading of 91.167 and 91.169 shows that the correct answer is that an alternate is always required unless the destination airport has a published approach and the weather meets the 1-2-3 rule. About 1 in 10 applicants have carefully read and understand that these two criteria are linked. This section is where the 800-2 non-precision approach and 600-2 precision approach weather requirements are set forth. You can also find the descent from MEA in VFR conditions to an alternate airport having no published approach requirement in this section. A lot of applicants confuse this with a destination airport having no published approach. Remember that if the destination airport has no published approach, the weather could be clear and 100sm visibility and an alternate would be required. The Airman's Information Manual, oops!! I am showing my age. The Aeronautical Information Manual (AIM) Chapter 1, Navigation Aids, has an excellent section explaining GPS. It is there that you find the note that an alternate airport cannot have a stand-alone GPS approach. It must have an approved ground based approach other than GPS or be treated as an airport with no published approach.

91.171 explains how to conduct a VOR receiver accuracy check. Applicants usually recite the requirements and how to do the check by rote. It becomes interesting when I ask how do you find the checkpoints to do the accuracy checks. Most applicants respond instantly with "They are in the AFD (Airport Facility Directory)." Then I ask them to show me where they are listed in the AFD.

It's hard to keep a straight face after watching the applicant spend five minutes of paging through the AFD airport directory and then the applicant says he, "Can't seem to find them." It's obvious that the applicant hasn't ever looked them up before I asked the question. Unbelievably more than one fourth the applicants can't accomplish this simple request.

AIRPORT/FACILITY DIRECTORY
SOUTHEAST U.S.

Effective 0901Z **5 APR 2012**
to 0901Z **31 MAY 2012**

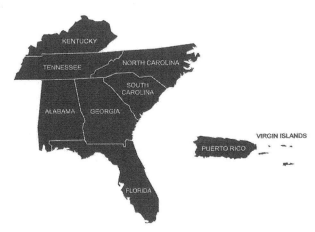

Consult NOTAMs for latest information
Warning: Refer to current foreign charts and flight information publications for information within foreign airspace
Published in accordance with specifications and agreements approved by the Federal Aviation Administration

Picture of an AFD

91.172 sets out the requirements regarding filing a flight plan and receiving a clearance to operate IFR in controlled airspace. Many applicants have trouble differentiating between Instrument Flight Rules (IFR) and Instrument Meteorological Conditions (IMC). This is probably due to the fact that the two terms are used interchangeably in conversation and many textbooks.

91.175 deals with takeoff and landing under IFR.

Paragraph (c) gives the requirements that must be met to operate below MDA or DH. Some applicants easily explain the three requirements but others stumble along and finally get it right. There is a lot of misunderstanding about the missed approach from an ILS approach. I point out that the aircraft descending on the glide slope has momentum that will cause the aircraft to continue to descend and inertia that must be overcome in order for it to begin to climb. Thus for a short time the aircraft has descended below the Decision Height/Decision Altitude. Is this okay? A lot of instrument applicants and instrument instructor applicants say no, you must never descend below the DH/DA unless landing. They carefully explain that you should begin leveling off about 100 high so as not to go below the minimum altitude. They don't get it. If you level off 100 feet high you will not cross the missed approach point at the correct altitude, instead having a full scale fly down indication which exceeds the allowed 3/4 scale deflection allowed by the Practical Test Standard (PTS) book. If the applicants had taken the time to read the PTS (now that's great idea, why don't applicants read it?), they would find statements like, "A missed approach or transition to landing shall be initiated at Decision Height," and, "initiates immediately the missed approach when at the DA/DH..."

Paragraph (f) sets out takeoff minimums for civil airports. Believe it or not, it doesn't directly address takeoffs under Part 91 operations. A lot of applicants, including instrument instructor, believe that the requirements are one sm visibility for aircraft having two engines or less and ½ sm for aircraft having more than two engines. These are the requirements for aircraft operated under Parts 121, 125, 129 and 135 at airports having no special takeoff procedures set out in Part 97. There is nothing said about Part 91 operations and it is widely interpreted to mean that Part 91 operators could take off under Zero/Zero conditions (Zero ceiling and zero visibility).

What is critical to Part 91 operators is an airport having special takeoff procedures. Consider Pompano Beach Airpark, Pompano Beach, Fl. The published takeoff minimums for Runway 15 (see US Terminal Procedures Southeast) are 400 foot ceiling and one sm visibility unless the aircraft can maintain a climb gradient of 300 feet per NM until 400 feet. I usually get the deer in the headlights look when I ask, "What is the climb rate in fpm required to meet the climb gradient?" No clue that there is a table on page D-1 of the Procedures where you can determine the needed climb rate or lacking the table you divide the climb gradient by 60 and multiply by your ground speed. Single engine aircraft like the Cessna 172 can easily make this climb requirement but what about the typical light twin such as the Piper Seminole and Beechcraft Duchess? Their single engine climb rate is about 200 fpm but the climb gradient requires their climb rate to be about 450fpm. Some departure procedures such as the Tampa Three Departure clearly state a required climb gradient. The TPA3 requires a climb gradient of 340 feet per nm up to 2600 feet for takeoff from Runway 18L. Amazingly some applicants think the gradient is required for all runways.

When I ask how could you safely depart from Runway 18L in a Piper Seminole or Beechcraft Duchess, they shrug their shoulders and mumble something about, "It isn't possible, you have to use a different runway." They miss the idea that taking off in VMC (visual metrological conditions) would be safe as you could make a visual return to the airport or visually maneuver to avoid the obstacles ahead. Nit-Picker Alert! The required performance numbers on these charts frequently change from issue to issue. The numbers used in this paragraph were accurate when I wrote it.

91.177 describes the minimum altitudes for IFR operation. Down here in Florida, most applicants overlook that in mountainous areas the minimum altitude is 2000 feet above the highest obstacle within four nm if there is no prescribed minimum altitude. The highest altitude on the Miami Sectional Chart is only 305 feet so the 2000 feet rule is moot in South Florida. This section also gives information about when to begin a climb to a higher MEA or approaching a MCA (Minimum Crossing Altitude) point.

91.179 and 181 describe the altitudes and course to be flown und IFR. Most applicants have little trouble with these two sections.

91.183 specifies IFR radio communication requirements. Although not set out in this section, this is a good spot to talk about how to make a position report. CFIs! Make your students read and understand AIM Chapter Five Section 5-3-2 titled, "Position Reporting" Especially read paragraph (d), Position Report Items. Perhaps the lack of knowledge in this area is because almost all of the student training is done under radar control here in South Florida It is rare that an applicant, including instrument instructors, can accurately explain how to make a correct position report.

91.185 IFR Operations: Two Way Radio Communications Failure

An instrument pilot should know this section better than the palm of his hand. Losing communications while flying in IMC is a very difficult emergency unless you know and understand how to apply the rules in this section.

A lot of applicants have memorized the loss of communication rules by rote using a favorite acronym, Avenue F, MEA.

Route to be flown:

A	Assigned Route
V	Vectors
E	Expected Route
F	Flight Plan Route

Altitude to be flown is the highest of the following:

M	Minimum En route Altitude
E	Expected Altitude
A	Assigned Altitude

Rote knowledge is a start. But it is best to test at the correlation level. During the oral portion of the practical test I review the student's cross country flight plan and eventually give him a clearance for his route of flight. A typical clearance from Pompano Beach Airpark to St. Petersburg-Clearwater International Airport would be something like this:

Cessna 12345 is cleared to the St. Petersburg-Clearwater International Airport via the Ft. Lauderdale Nine Departure, THNDR (pronounced Thunder) Transition, Victor 157 LaBelle, Victor 97, St. Petersburg Direct. Maintain 2000, expect 6000 ten minutes after departure. Departure frequency is 119.7. Squawk 3456.

As a side note, I see some amazing chicken scratching that masquerades as copying a clearance. What ever happened to the old saying, "Cleanliness is next to Godliness?" Learn how to copy neatly. So you can understand it five minutes after you wrote it.

I then set up the scenario. From the Georgia border south, the weather is 800 feet overcast and the visibility is two sm. Cloud tops are 15,000. Pompano Tower says, "After takeoff fly heading 090." We takeoff and passing through 1500 feet are instructed to contact Miami Departure. We cannot raise them and determine that we have had a total communications failure and cannot restore communications. My question to the instrument applicant is, "What should we do next?" and to the instrument instructor applicant is, "Teach me what to do next." Almost everyone remembers to set their transponder to code 7600. Then comes divergence from the correct procedure.

The all time best answer to the question came from an instrument applicant. He said he would reach into his flight bag and pull out his handheld communications radio, which also was able to navigate using GPS. I told him good thinking but I wanted to find out his knowledge of 91.185.

Some of the more interesting answers were, "I know that I am over the ocean so I will let down until I see the water and return to Pompano VFR."

Another was, "I will fly direct to THNDR Intersection and then continue as cleared." I told the applicant that this would be a good trick going direct to THNDR since his aircraft was equipped only with two VOR receivers, one ADF and a Transponder, and had no GPS or DME.

Another applicant heard a voice from the past and said he would, "Fly a triangle pattern for two minutes before proceeding on course." I have no idea what he meant by proceeding on course.

The well trained applicants correctly explain that the Ft. Lauderdale Nine Departure must be reviewed before takeoff and that the THNDR Transition starts over the Dolphin (DHP) VOR and after going overhead DHP follow the 335 radial to THNDR.

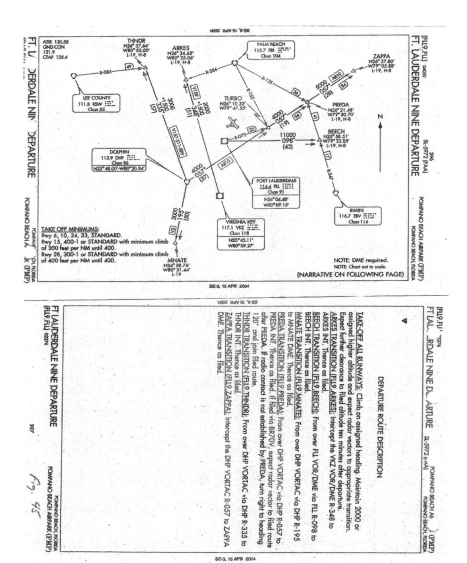

Ft. Lauderdale Nine departure

The next problem is what altitude to maintain. The rules solve every contingency. Maintain 2000 for 10 minutes and then climb to 6000 unless a MEA higher than 2000 is encountered before 10 minutes has passed. AIM Chapter Six, Section Four, explains the loss of communications rules and has some examples. It is amazing how many applicants have no idea that this information is in the AIM.

The final problem I give occurs upon arrival in the vicinity of the destination. I pose this question. "How do you propose to make your landing at St. Petersburg Clearwater International Airport?"

A very popular answer is, "I will hold until my ETA occurs, then make a landing." Many applicants say that they will proceed to LAFAL Intersection for their holding. They explain that the intersection is the holding point for the missed approach and they will not interfere with other traffic if they hold, "out of the way." Another popular fix to hold at is the St. Petersburg VOR. Some applicants think they should hold at the Final Approach Fix.

When I ask, "Why hold at all?," the holding fraternity says that you must hold until your ETA before starting an approach as stated in the FARs. So far no one has been able to show me that citation. I then ask them whether or not you can proceed to your clearance limit without any holding prior to arrival at the clearance limit. Most will say yes. I then ask them what did they copy as their clearance limit. Unable to decipher their chicken scratch masquerading as a clearance, I remind them that their clearance limit was the airport. If they want to circle until their ETA, after landing they could request taxi clearance to a remote parking area and circle around on the ground.

The confusion is caused by lack of English skills. The misunderstood citation is 91.185 (3), Leave Clearance Limit. Paragraph (i) states, "When the clearance limit is a fix from which an approach begins..." Obviously the airport is where the approach ends, not begins, so this paragraph does not apply. Paragraph (ii) states, "When the clearance limit is not a fix from which an approach begins, leave the clearance limit at the expect further clearance time if one has been received, or if none has been received, upon arrival over the clearance limit proceed to a fix from which an approach begins and commence descent and approach as close as possible to the estimated time of arrival..." Why would you leave the airport after you arrived to do an approach at ETA? A silly but sad commentary on the state of our population's English skills and a lack of IFR procedures knowledge. To wit, "You can proceed to your clearance limit without holding delay." Think. Does ATC want you holding in the Terminal Area and interfering with other traffic? Have you ever received a clearance that did not clear you to an airport? There must be a reason!

The last problem for the applicant is when to begin descent. Some want to figure out a time and distance calculation from cruise to initial approach altitude and start down on the airway being careful not to descend below MEA. The proper procedure is that you may start down when you begin the approach. If you are on a Feeder Route you may start down. If you arrive at the Final Approach Fix (FAF) too high, hold on the procedure turn side and continue descent until reaching the FAF altitude. The correct solution to how to make a landing at St. Petersburg in this situation is to select an approach that begins at the St. Petersburg VOR (PIE) and then fly the approach.

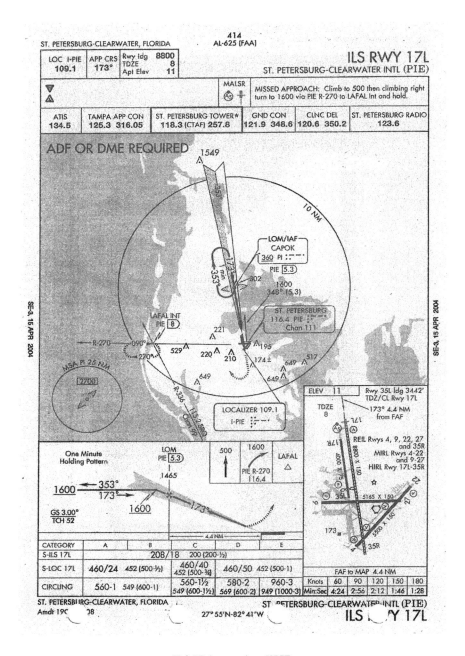

ILS 17 Approach at KPIE

91.187 covers malfunction reports. Most applicants have no problems with this.

91.189, 191 and 193 cover Category II operations and usually are not covered in detail during an instrument practical test. It's 'good enough' if the applicant knows that Category II requires special aircraft equipment and pilot qualification.

The Instrument Flight Test

I've seen some truly amazing flying techniques during the flight portion of the instrument practical test. Some of them have been shuffled to the, "You're Too Dtupid to Be a Pilot" chapter. Here are some tests that don't quite measure up to inclusion in that chapter.

There is a reason that the FAA included interception and tracking of radials in the six-month IFR currency requirements. Many pilots need to continuously review and practice these procedures because they don't understand the basic principles of tracking VOR radials I usually give a clearance similar to this during the flight test, "Intercept the Palm Beach (PBI) VOR 210 degree radial and proceed inbound." Many applicants start by turning the Omni Bearing Selector (OBS) until they get the Course Deviation Indicator (CDI) to center with a FROM indication They announce that we are on that radial (say they have identified the 220 degree radial) and then reset the OBS to the 210 degree radial. The CDI will present a, "Fly Left" indication and the applicant will turn left to the west in an attempt to intercept the radial, which is the wrong way to turn because they are now going away from the PBI VOR. Eventually they realize that they must turn further to the left and fly southbound until they reach the 210-degree radial and the CDI centers. I remember one applicant who made a 360-degree circle before he got established on the 210-degree radial. Then the applicant continued to the southwest away from the PBI VOR. I asked him how much fuel was on board as we had a trip ahead of us of at least 25,000 nm. They are clueless as how to carry out this basic ATC instruction. About half of the test failures are due to inability to intercept and track.

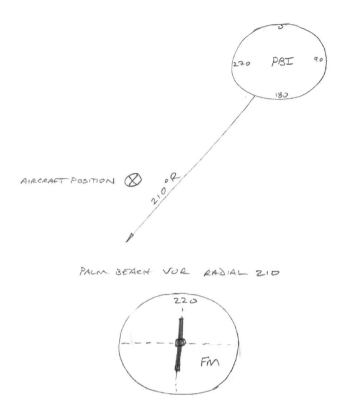

Diagram Showing PBI Radial 210 and OBS 220 Setting

What could be simpler than setting the reciprocal of the 210-degree radial from, the 030 radial TO, as the first step and then orient yourself with the PBI VOR? If you see a left needle then you have to fly left to intercept the 030 radial and a right needle requires you to fly right to intercept. How can the applicants continue to miss that the instruction to fly inbound requires that the OBS show a TO indication?

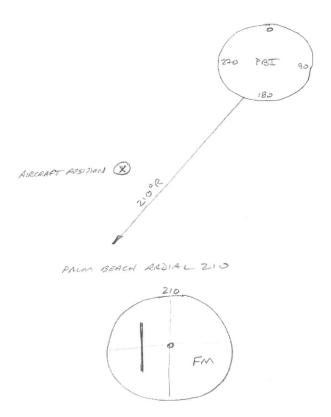

Diagram Showing PBI Radial 210 and OBS 210 Setting

Another variation on interception and tracking was a clearance to, "Fly heading 290, intercept PBI radial 230 and proceed to NEWER intersection." The instrument applicant tuned and identified PBI and set 230 on the OBS. Then the applicant turned to a heading of 060. After five miles of this I asked, "What are you doing?"

The applicant said, "I am flying to PBI and then I will track the 230 radial to NEWER." How do you explain making up your own clearance?

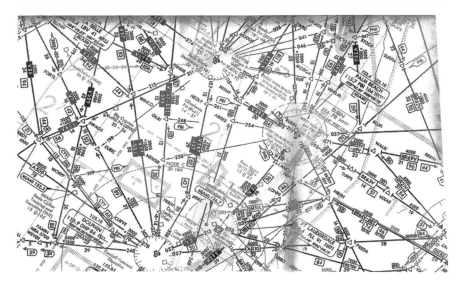

Portion of En Route Chart Showing PBI and
NEWER and Aircraft Starting Point

The instrument applicant was given a clearance to maintain 3000 feet and proceed direct to the Pahokee VOR (PHK) then to JATEL intersection and hold as published. (View the approach plate for the PHK VOR-DME -A approach) After reaching the PHK VOR the applicant flew the heading of 002 degrees instead of tracking the 002 radial. In addition the applicant had set the OBS (omni bearing selector) to 182 degrees, which was 180 degrees out of phase with the tracking to JATEL. There was a wind from the east so the airplane was blown off to the west. It took the applicant 3 circuits to get established in the hold. The applicant was then cleared to descend to 2000 feet and received clearance for the VOR-DME(A) approach. As soon as the applicant intercepted the 182 radial inbound north of JATEL he began descending and crossed JATEL intersection at 1000 feet.

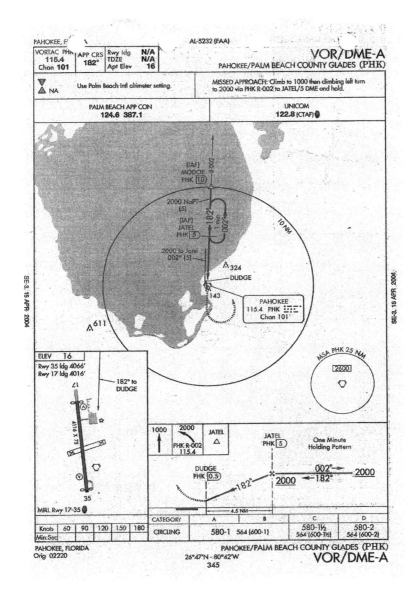

Pahokee VOR-DME (A) Approach Plate

Another instrument candidate showed absolute evil genius regarding the Pahokee VOR-DME (A) approach. He noted that the final inbound course was not aligned with Runway 17. He asked, "Could you use local knowledge and fly offset the final course to be aligned with the runway?" I asked him how he could do it. What VOR radial would he use? Or would he use the GPS? His solution was "Fly with the about one half scale needle deflection and that would keep you just west of course." I asked him why he would use one half-scale deflection. He replied, "Because the PTS limit is three quarter scale deflection." At least he knew the PTS passing minimum standard.

A CFI-IA candidate was demonstrating how to make a parallel entry into a holding pattern. The way the intersection hold was being entered required a left hand turn for the parallel entry but the candidate made a right hand turn into the non-holding side of the holding radial. Turning the wrong way is instant failure for a CFI-IA candidate.

I noticed an Instrument Airplane applicant was sweating profusely and was pale in color. I offered the applicant a Letter of Discontinuance but he declined. He didn't seem to understand so I explained to him two times that a Letter of Discontinuance was like getting an incomplete, and that we could continue the fight test another day. Soon thereafter I saw him holding his stomach and noted he was bathed in sweat. I recommended to him that we stop the test due to his condition. He insisted that we continue saying that he, "Wanted to get the rating today." ATC gave him a vector to intercept the localizer, which he turned to but he failed to see the localizer needle center and flew through the course. He reached full-scale deflection and still had no idea what had happened. During the debrief I inquired about his physical condition. He said had eaten bad food at dinner the evening before and had no sleep the night before the test and had not eaten any breakfast that morning. Once again the basic training about being fit for flight had been ignored with resulting failure. Fortunately it was only failure of a flight test, not an accident. This one almost made the, "You're Too Stupid to Be a Pilot," chapter.

A lady applicant was wearing shoes with substantial platform soles. You know the kind, like elevator shoes. We were landing from a circling approach and after touchdown the aircraft veered towards the runway edge. She shouted. "I can't control the airplane!" Because of our predicament, heading for the grass and beginning to bounce, I took control, applied full power, back elevator and full right rudder to correct the flight path and make a go around. She began screaming in pain. When we reached a safe altitude I investigated why she was screaming and found that somehow she had tangled her right foot and platform shoe beneath the rudder pedal and couldn't get it free. I had to get off the pedals and help her extricate her foot.

Short distance non-precision approaches present a problem for many applicants who are locked into robotic flying like always descending at 500 fpm because that's what the instructor taught. A case in point was an applicant who was flying the VOR RWY 15 at Lantana Airport (LNA). The applicant didn't recognize a tailwind on the approach and dutifully descended at his ingrained 500 fpm rate. He passed over the airport well before time expired and when he looked out he could not see the airport as it was a considerable distance behind him. This could haves been avoided if he had backed up his timing with the DME which is more exact than the timing, recognized that he had a faster than normal ground speed, and increased his descent rate to compensate. He also forgot to set up the #2 VOR to the PHK VOR to identify the missed approach holding fix and didn't realize that he could have used the PBI DME to also identify the holding fix.

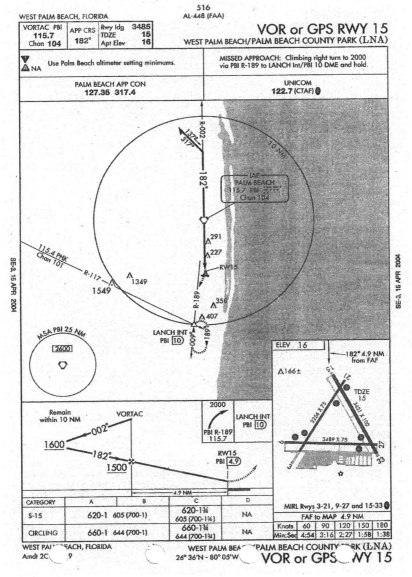

Lantana VOR RWY 15 Approach Plate

Another applicant had a fixation on flying a heading of 090 degrees. He was cleared direct to the PBI VOR and then the VOR RWY 15 to LNA. He was told to report the procedure turn inbound. When we reached the PBI VOR he turned to a heading of 090 degrees and started to report his procedure turn inbound. We immediately corrected that error as Palm Beach Approach runs a very busy airspace and can't tolerate gross errors. After the approach was made we continued with the missed approach procedure. When we reached LANCH intersection (the holding fix) the applicant made a turn to 090 degrees and then announced that he had turned the wrong way. I suggested that since we were on the correct side of the holding course he could recover with a teardrop entry. He turned to a heading of 150 degrees and flew for one minute and then turned to a heading of 090 degrees. I couldn't take any more and stopped the test.

It must be something about LANCH. An instrument airplane applicant successfully completed the VOR RWY 15 approach and then began the missed approach procedure. He crossed LANCH and made a parallel entry into the holding pattern. When he got back to LANCH he failed to see that he was there and continued to fly north until he was back overhead Lantana airport. I asked him why the DME reading was so low and why he had a full deflection on the PHK VOR course that defines LANCH.

His answer? "Does that mean I fail?"

Another instrument applicant was being vectored to the final approach course for the Pompano Airpark Localizer 15 (LOC-15) approach. We were approaching from the north and the controller said to fly a heading of 180 degrees to intercept the localizer. Just as the localizer needle came alive (began to move from full right deflection towards the center point) the applicant remembered that he had to identify the signal. For non pilots, navigation signals have a three or four letter identification signal broadcast in Morse code so the pilot can be sure that the navigation facility is operational, and that he has the correct station selected by listening to the Morse code signal. The applicant tried to identify the localizer (I-PMP frequency 109.75) by listening to the communication radio. The type of radio he was using has two volume control knobs, one for communication, and the other for navigation. He had the navigation knob at silent position and the communication knob at full volume position. After a minute or so the applicant said, "I can't hear the ident because the tower is talking too much." While this was taking place he forgot about navigating and flew through the course on the 180-degree heading getting a full-scale deflection of the course needle to the left. Since the PTS standard is ¾ scale deflection of the navigation needle there was no choice but to give him a Notice of Disapproval.

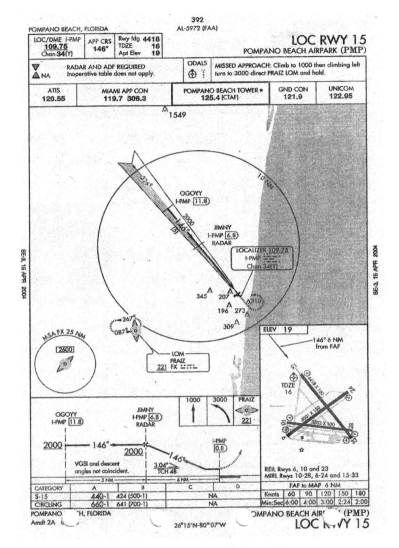

Pompano Airpark Localizer 15 Approach Plate

An instrument applicant was attempting to fly the LOC RWY 15 approach at Pompano. He forgot to listen to the ATIS, which provides important information about the airport such as current weather, approach in use, runway in use and any known hazards. If he had listened he would have learned that the landing runway was Runway 10 and that circling minimums (660 feet) would apply. He provided no approach briefing. Maybe he would have caught himself and listened to the ATIS but he did not. He was flying a Cessna 172, which normally is flown on approach at 90 knots. This applicant crossed the final fix (JIMNY) at 120 knots and maintained that speed throughout the approach. Not the best idea but not an automatic failure if he used the 120-knot time for the approach.

As we crossed JIMNY the Approach Controller said, "Cleared for the Localizer 15 Approach circle to Runway 10, and contact Pompano Tower." The applicant read back the clearance and continued the approach. The tower said to begin circling at I-95 and report on left base for Runway 10. The applicant read back that clearance. After we leveled at 440 feet I asked the applicant which runway we using.

He said, "I'm doing the Localizer to Runway 15." I then asked him if he had forgotten that we were circling to Runway 10. He said, "Uh-Oh." Then I told him to turn right and enter a left base for Runway 10. Much to my amazement he then started searching through his navigation charts looking for the Pompano airport diagram. When he finally looked outside he was lost. The airport was behind us as he had let the airplane turn 90 degrees to the right. Whatever happened to common sense?

Here is some information for non-pilots: The radio navigation indicators have little red flags that appear and say OFF when no signal is being received. This is one way the pilot is alerted that he should not continue navigating with that frequency. When flying a precision approach (an ILS) you have two position needles to control, the localizer signal (lateral guidance) and the glide-slope signal (vertical guidance). You watch for two flags, one for the localizer and one for the glide-slope.

Picture of Navigation Head Showing Two OFF Flags

During an instrument flight test the applicant was flying the ILS RWY 8R at North County Airport (F45). Shortly after beginning descent on the glide-slope, the glide-slope transmitter at the airport failed and an OFF flag appeared on the navigation head. The applicant did not see the OFF flag and continued to descend. The glide-slope indicator needle stayed in the center failed position giving no guidance.

After awhile I said, "You're doing an amazing job of tracking the glide-slope."

He answered, "Yeah, that's one of the things that I do best." Then I told him to look outside and explain how we could be 1000 feet above the airport with a centered glide-slope needle.

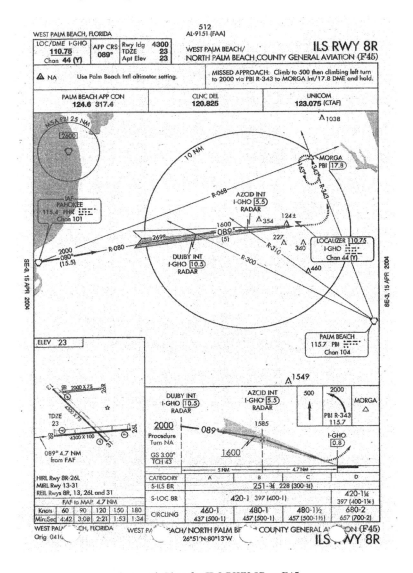

Approach Plate for ILS RWY 8R at F45

Another applicant had interesting variation of this. After he tuned in the localizer frequency and identified it, he continued on with the ILS approach. He never saw the glide-slope OFF flag. It was showing OFF from the moment he selected the ILS frequency. The glide-slope indicator needle was at the top of the instrument and moved down to the center position as you would expect on normal intercept. Then the needle began to oscillate up and down at times reaching ½ scale deflections. The applicant dutifully followed the indicator. When it was apparent that we would impact the ground about 1 mile short of the runway I asked the applicant to look out the front window.

He said, "What happened?" I asked him if he had seen the OFF flag for the glide-slope.

He replied, "Yes I saw it, but the needle seemed to be working OK." He had no clue that a glide-slope needle would never continually oscillate between ½ scale up and ½ scale down deflections unless there was something not right.

Certified Flight Instructors

You would think that by the time a pilot reaches the point in his career when he applies to become a certified flight instructor (CFI), he would be over the dumb mistakes of low time pilots. This chapter will amaze you and disappoint you. It is amazing and it is disappointing in that some of our CFIs have such poor knowledge, poor piloting skills, and poor ability to teach.

The practical test for the initial CFI certificate is difficult. There is a huge amount of knowledge required of the applicant who must also demonstrate that he can teach it. The oral portion of the practical test is long and probing. For example, after the applicant explains a particular maneuver, he must also be able to explain common student errors and how to correct them. The flight portion covers many maneuvers. The applicant must be able to simultaneously perform a maneuver within Practical Test Standards while providing instruction as to how to fly the maneuver. For some applicants the instruction part is the most difficult part of the test. They cannot fly and teach at the same time. Performing the maneuver takes all of their attention.

Here is an example of what I am talking about. An applicant for CFI-ASE (Airplane Single Engine) was asked to teach how to make a short field landing over an obstacle. He performed the maneuver very good but after our landing I told him he had flown the entire maneuver in silence and a student would not have gained too much from his teaching. He replied, "I don't know what to say." This could have been a problem with his instruction for the CFI certificate. Perhaps his instructor failed to provide training regarding to how to verbally instruct while performing a maneuver.

I have organized this chapter by three of the possible flight instructor ratings, Airplane Single Engine (ASE), Instrument Airplane (IA) and Airplane Multiengine (AME). This is the normal order of obtaining the CFI ratings although some schools start with the IA or AME depending on their course syllabus.

Airplane Single Engine

The applicant was asked to demonstrate how to use an E6-B computer to compute crosswind correction angle and ground speed during cross-country flight planning. For non-pilots the E6-B is a wonderful manual computer that has been in aviation since the 1930s. On one side you can easily compute crosswind correction angle and ground speed when planning a cross-country flight. The other side is a circular slide rule with many functions. You can compute density altitude, flight time, fuel consumption, change unit of measure basis between stature miles, nautical miles and kilometers, and determine true airspeed. One of the best features is that the E6-B has no batteries. It can't fail. This applicant did not have an E6-B so I lent him mine. The applicant could not perform the most basic functions using an E6-B. He could only use an electronic flight-planning computer that he had brought with him. The applicant said he had never used an E6-B and had no idea how to use it. So here is a pilot who has spent his entire piloting career pushing buttons on a hand held computer when doing flight planning and never learned how to use the most basic piece of equipment that most students learn to use before they fly solo cross country.

I asked the applicant, "How do you expect to be a CFI if you can't use an E6-B?" I received a rambling answer about how an E6-B was from prehistoric times and students should be trained with modern equipment.

Pictures of E6-B Front and Back

An ASE applicant was asked to explain the airport information for Boca Raton Airport (KBCT) as shown on the Miami Sectional navigation chart.

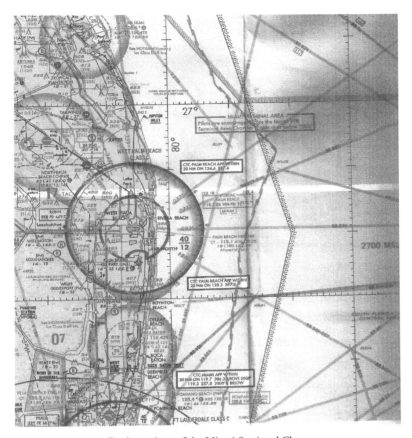

Pertinent Area of the Miami Sectional Chart

The correct explanation would be as follows:

Boca Raton	Boca Raton	Name of airport
BCT	ICAO code	Airport identification code
CT-118.425* C	Control Tower	Frequency 118.425
		*Means a part time tower C
		Means common traffic advisory frequency when the tower is closed
13	Airport elevation	Airport height above sea level
*L	Runway lights	*Means part time lighting pilot controlled
62	Longest runway	Longest runway is 6200 feet
122.8	Unicom	Frequency for the FBO
RP23	Right traffic 23	Runway 23 has right traffic pattern

The applicant thought the *C meant the type of control tower, Federal or Private employees, the *L meant that Runway 13 normally had left hand traffic but sometimes it was right hand traffic, the 62 was the airport elevation and that frequency 122.8 was a backup frequency for the control tower. He had no idea what the RP23 meant. He thought the star on top of the airport indicated that fuel was available. He was really flustered when I pointed out that there were only Runways 5 and 23 at Boca Raton, and the star on top of the airport symbol meant that there was a rotating beacon at night. How did he expect to pass that day? I wouldn't let a student solo if he didn't know how to decipher the airport information shown on the Sectional Chart.

Another ASE candidate was asked how to communicate with frequency 122.1R in the vicinity of the LaBelle VOR.

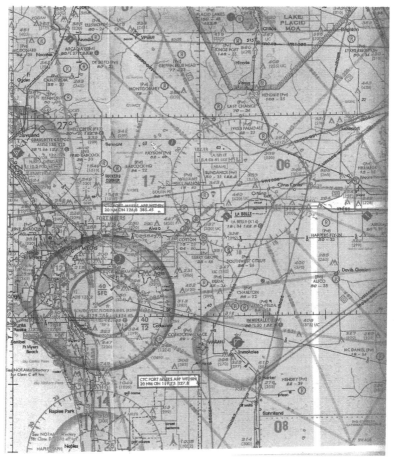

Pertinent Area of the Miami Sectional Chart

The applicant explained that to contact Miami Center in the vicinity of the LaBelle VOR you would transmit on frequency 110.4 and receive on frequency 122.1. I asked the applicant to explain how to transmit on frequency 110.4. He said to tune frequency 110.4 into the communication radio and use the push to talk switch. Then I pointed out that the communication radio frequencies started at 118.0 and went higher. I also pointed out on a cockpit diagram that the transmitter selector switch only had a Com 1 and Com 2 position. After a lot of tap dancing by the applicant I explained that frequency 122.1R was a one-way frequency and that when we transmitted on that frequency in the vicinity of the LaBelle VOR, Miami Flight Service Station would hear us and would respond on the VOR frequency 110.4; another CFI applicant who didn't know basic information needed by a student pilot before going solo.

Both of the above applicants lived to fight another day. They studied the Sectional Chart symbols and did just fine on their retest. In case you are wondering, they failed for many more reasons than messing up a chart symbol. Both had disturbingly poor knowledge about information depicted on Sectional Charts. It is a depressing situation that many of the CFI applicants either never learned or have forgotten how to read a Sectional Chart. A lot of CFI check-rides are failed because of this.

Another ASE applicant was teaching how to preflight a Cessna 172 RG. He forgot to test the stall warning system. The test is simple. Turn on the electrical power with the master switch and then go to the leading edge of the left wing and move the stall-warning vane. If the stall warning system is working you will hear a horn. As the applicant prepared to read the Before Start checklist I asked the applicant if he had completed the Preflight checklist. He said he had completed it. I then asked about the stall warning test that was part of the Preflight checklist.

He said, "Oops! I forgot to do it."

An ASE started a Cessna 172 RG and prepared to taxi. He advanced the throttle but the airplane didn't move. He tried full power but the airplane still didn't move. Then I asked him why he hadn't removed the tail tie down rope.

An ASE started a Cessna 172 RG and prepared to taxi. He failed to notice that the red low voltage warning light was illuminated. During the before takeoff checks he tested the electrical system by turning the landing light on and checking the ammeter for a discharge. He failed to notice that the ammeter was indicating a discharge before he turned the landing light on and only saw that the ammeter needle moved left when the landing light was on and moved right when the landing light was turned off. He didn't see the red low voltage warning light that was located within two inches of the ammeter. As he prepared to call for takeoff clearance I told him to get taxi clearance back to the parking ramp.

He said, 'Why?"

I pointed to the red low voltage light.

He said, "Does that mean I fail?"

I asked him what was the procedure to follow when the low voltage warning light illuminated.

He said, "Land as soon as possible."

I suggested that he might want to look up the procedure in the Operating Handbook Emergency Procedures chapter before the next check-ride. It is beyond belief that almost no applicant knows that there is a procedure to follow when the Low Voltage light illuminates in a Cessna single engine airplane.

Part of the preflight briefing for an ASE applicant included a caution, "Do not inadvertently fly into a cloud during a maneuver." The weather conditions that day were scattered clouds at 2000 feet. After takeoff during the initial climb out I cautioned the applicant that he appeared to be closer than 2000 feet horizontally from a passing cloud. Later, during the test I again cautioned that we were getting too close to the clouds. Still later into the test I asked the applicant to demonstrate how to handle an engine out emergency. The applicant simulated an engine failure by retarding the throttle to idle and began descending for an emergency landing in a field below. As we descended we entered a cloud. I asked why we were going through a cloud. The applicant said, "I have an emergency." He was oblivious to the fact that he could have easily modified his descent to avoid to the cloud.

An ASE departed KPMP taking off on Runway 28. After performing some maneuvers I asked the applicant to show me how to find Belle Glade Airport (X10) by pilotage and then demonstrate a short field landing. On the way to X10 we heard an aircraft at Immokolee Airport (KIMM) announcing that they were using Runway 27. X10 is about halfway between IMM and PMP. Slightly northeast from X10 is a sugar refining plant. The smoke from the stacks clearly indicated that the wind was from the west. The applicant landed on Runway 9 with a strong tailwind. I inquired why he had landed on Runway 9 instead of Runway 27. He said, "I've always landed on Runway 9 here."

The final ASE example is a 180-degree accuracy landing. For non-pilots this is a maneuver that requires knowledge of the airplane's performance, and the ability to accurately plan and fly a glide path to the runway. The landing gear is extended on the downwind leg of the traffic pattern and opposite the touchdown point the throttle is retarded to idle. One of the Practical Test Standards requirements for this maneuver is to touch down not before and no more than 200 feet past a specified point on the runway. This applicant misjudged his descent and was going to be short of the runway. He started pulling up on the yoke in an attempt to stretch his glide to the runway. It was obvious that we were going to touchdown in the grass 25 feet short of the runway. Instead of going around, the applicant pulled back more in an attempt to make it to the pavement. Just before touchdown in the grass I took control of the airplane and initiated a go around. The applicant insisted, "I could have made it." He wasn't ready to be a CFI.

Instrument Airplane

I caution the CFI-IA applicants that their flying must be perfect. If the entry into a holding pattern should be a left turn and they turn right, then they will not pass. If the crossing altitude at the Final Fix inbound is 2000 feet and they cross at 1800 feet they will not pass. If they miss a radio call from ATC they will not pass. If they incorrectly tune radios they will not pass. Some CFI-IA material is included in the Instrument Airplane chapter and will not be repeated here.

The IA applicant was demonstrating how to fly the LOC-15 at Pompano Beach Airpark. He tuned in the localizer frequency of 109.75 (I-PMP) in the navigation radio but forgot to switch it from standby position to active position. He dutifully checked the Morse Code identification signal and continued with the approach. The problem was that he had listened to the active frequency, 115.4 (PHK), the Pahokee VOR identifier. He was approaching the final inbound course from the west and flew through the course waiting for the CDI to center. As we passed over the beach I told him to look outside and explain how we had gone so far east of course. He said, "I have no idea. The needle should have centered by now."

Another IA applicant was demonstrating how to fly the ILS-12 at Opa Locka Airport (KOPF).

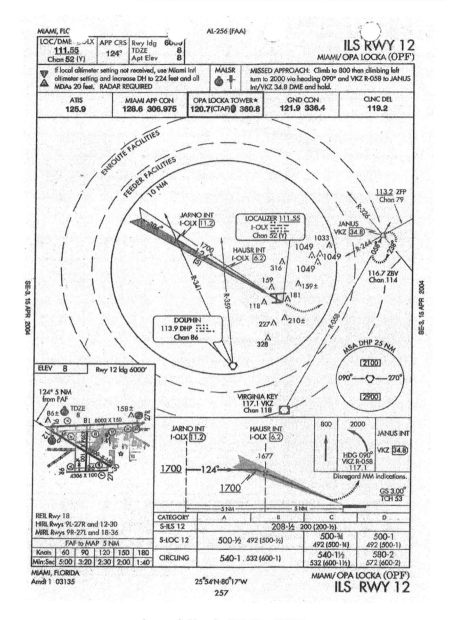

Approach Plate for ILS-12 at KOPF

The applicant tuned in frequency 111.50 instead of the correct frequency of 111.55. He listened for the Morse Code identifier without success. He said, "We are too far out to receive the signal." The Approach Controller gave us a final intercept vector. I mentioned that the OFF flag was still showing. The applicant said, "There must be a problem with the station. We should call Approach Control."

I asked why the DME had not been tuned for the approach.

He said, "We don't need it."

I asked what was the DME frequency.

The applicant looked at the approach chart and said, "How could I have been so stupid? Did I fail?"

After takeoff and flying out to the practice area we finished the IFR air work and began the navigation phase. The applicant admitted that he had not brought any en route charts or the approach plate book. He only had, "The charts for approaches you said we might do."

I said, "How can you instruct en route procedures without an en route chart? Return to the airport."

He said, "Does that mean I fail?" Another candidate for the, "You're Too Stupid," chapter.

An IA candidate was showing how to hold at NEWER Intersection on Airway Victor 157 northwest with one-minute right hand turns. NEWER is defined by the 335-degree radial from the Dolphin VOR (DHP) and the 230-degree radial from the Palm Beach VOR (PBI).

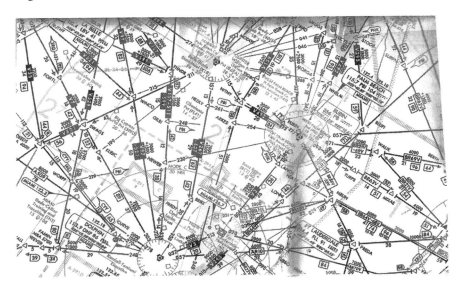

Excerpt from En Route Chart L-19 Showing NEWER

He tuned number one navigation radio to frequency 113.9 for DHP, but forgot to switch it from standby to active. He already had number two navigation radio tuned to 115.7 for PBI. He pushed the button on the number one navigation radio to show the radial from the station, which puts the radial number in place of the standby VOR frequency. He had the number one navigation radioactive on frequency 114.4, the Ft. Lauderdale VOR (FLL). He listened to the FLL Morse Code and said he had identified DHP. When he thought it was time to turn inbound to DHP he said we had to reset the number one OBS to the inbound course of 155 degrees to have correct sensing. Instead he reset the OBS for the number two navigation radio, which was tuned to PBI from 230 degrees to to 155 degrees. I asked how he knew when to turn inbound. He said that we had flown north enough time after passing the PBI 230 degree radial. Lost in space without a clue.

Another IA candidate was demonstrating the same hold at NEWER intersection. He was established on V-157 northbound approaching the intersection. He failed to see when he passed the PBI 230 degree radial and continued northbound for 10 miles. He didn't use the DME or the GPS to determine his position relative to DHP. Finally, I told him we had gone north of the intersection and he reversed course. Then he again failed to see the OBS center on the PBI 230-degree radial and continued past it heading south. When we were three miles south of NEWER I told him the check-ride was over for the day.

Another disaster at NEWER. This applicant successfully tuned both navigation radios to DHP and PBI and set the DME to the DHP frequency. He set the wrong radial for PBI. As we crossed what he thought was the NEWER intersection, I asked him why the DME was indicating two miles different from the charted distance while the PBI OBS was centered. He said, "The DME station must be in error."

Another favorite mistake by many IA applicants when holding at an intersection is to enter the intersection into the GPS and fly direct to the intersection. The plan is to then get established on the VOR holding radial and continue with the entry procedure. Many times the airplane intercepts the holding radial before reaching the intersection. Unfortunately there are times when the GPS intersection position does not coincide with the VOR intersection position. So the applicant flies on by the intersection passing it by 0.5 mile or so, never noticing that the distance is now getting bigger. The applicant will still be waiting for the GPS distance to count down to zero miles.

Almost no CFI-IA candidate can explain the discrepancy between the GPS and the VOR position. It's really straight forward if you understand the basics of VORs. We test our VORs for accuracy every 30 days. The tolerance is plus or minus four degrees when tested against each other. A rule of thumb is that if you are one degree off course at 60 miles from the VOR, then you are 1 mile off course. Thus if your VOR is off one degree and the intersection is 30 miles from the VOR, you will be 0.5 mile off course. The GPS is very accurate. It is easy to have a 0.5 mile discrepancy between your VOR position and your GPS position. The least confusing way to handle an intersection hold is to use the VOR radial for the course, and set the GPS to the VOR and use it like a DME.

The final IA example involves intercepting and tracking a radial. The task was to intercept the Pahokee VOR (PHK) 140-degree radial and proceed inbound. The instruction provided was to center the OBS to determine what

PHK radial we were currently on, which was found to be the 160-degree radial. The applicant then said we should fly a course of 090 to intercept the 140-degree radial. I didn't say anything even though the 090 course was taking us away from PHK and the quickest intercept angle would be a course of 050. Then when we intercepted the 140-degree radial the applicant left the OBS set to 140 degrees and flew inbound to PHK using reverse sensing. He should have reset the OBS to 320 degrees for correct sensing. This is basic Private Pilot stuff. Do applicants just forget their previous training?

Airplane Multiengine

Applicants for the CFI-Airplane Multiengine (AME) certificate fail for a variety of reasons but a majority of failures are due to the following:
- Poor knowledge regarding a variety of topics evidenced by reading answers to questions from notes, not speaking from what is in their mind
- Unfamiliar with FAR Part 61 requirements for CFI-AME and multiengine ratings
- Weak explanations of multiengine aerodynamics
- Unable to teach weight and balance procedures
- Lack of understanding Sectional Chart symbols
- Flight maneuver demonstrations outside PTS standards
- Unable to use all equipment installed in the test airplane

Now for some examples:

A candidate for Commercial Pilot Airplane Multiengine Land presented his logbook for review. He showed me in his logbook a 3.2 hour day VFR dual cross country trip to satisfy the 2.0 hour day dual VFR requirement. He and his instructor had logged 2.0 hours of actual instrument time on the trip. That trip was not acceptable. (Note: Since this check-ride the FAR has been changed to allow instrument time on the 2.0 hour day and 2.0 hour night dual cross country trips). His night dual VFR cross country trip lasted 2.8 hours, but he and his instructor had logged 1.4 hours of actual instrument time. Another unacceptable trip.

The Commercial Pilot long cross-country trip requirement is a trip of at least 300 nautical miles with landings at three points one of which is a straight line distance of at least 250 nautical miles from the origination point. This applicant had a trip from Opa-Locka (OPF) to LaBelle (LBV) to Lakeland (LAL) to Cross City (CTY). OPF to LBV is 85 nm, LBV to LAL is 80 nm and LAL to CTY is 105 nm making a total trip length of 270 nm. Another unacceptable trip.

Then I looked at the application (Form 8710). The application had been, 'signed' by another examiner before I saw the 8710 but the date of signing and oral exam and the flight test times had not been filled in. I contacted the recommending instructor and read him the riot act, especially about the examiner signature. He claimed he knew nothing about it. The applicant claimed the other examiner had signed the application and then had to postpone the test and the applicant had then found me. I told the applicant not to comeback after he did his cross-country flights but to go back to the other examiner, And that was the end of that. How sad that the instructor didn't know the Part 61 requirements and that cost the student a lot of money repeating the cross-country flights.

An applicant who was using a Piper Seminole (PA-44) was asked to teach how to compute a weight and balance problem. The two pilots had a total weight of 400 pounds and there were 12 small boxes weighing 50 pounds each. The applicant computed the weight and balance. He said we couldn't go because the gross weight was 300 pounds over the maximum allowed. He couldn't reduce the fuel because the school policy was to never take off with less than full fuel.

A second applicant had the same assignment. He decided to leave some boxes behind. After spending 20 more minutes of trial and error calculating, he was unable to recompute the new center of gravity.

A third try. This applicant put all the boxes (600 pounds) in the baggage area. He was oblivious to the limitation of 200 pounds maximum in the baggage compartment. He never thought about putting 400 pounds on the rear seats. After he realized he was overweight he reduced the fuel to 400 pounds and split the boxes to 300 pounds on the rear seats and 300 pounds in the baggage area. He spent 40 minutes mumbling to himself completely occupied with his calculator and never giving anything resembling instruction. He never solved the problem.

A fourth applicant tried the same problem. He finished his demonstration and said, "Uh-oh. We're overweight." He decided to remove some fuel. He said there was a formula he could use to determine how much fuel to remove. He said "X" was the amount to remove, but he couldn't remember the rest of the formula. Then he looked up weight and balance in his textbook and showed me three formulas for adding, subtracting, and moving weight but he couldn't decide which formula to use. All of this had taken 30 minutes. I then suggested that he subtract the Zero Fuel Weight (aircraft empty weight plus people and cargo) from the Maximum Takeoff Weight to see how much fuel we could take. He was in total amazement as to how simple it was.

A fifth applicant saw no problem taking off 300 pounds overweight. He said it was an unwritten rule that you could takeoff 10% higher than maximum takeoff weight. Thus, if the maximum allowed takeoff weight was 3800 pounds there would be no problem taking off at 4100 pounds as we were under the 10% overage limit by 80 pounds. I was speechless. Where do these ideas come from?

A CFI-AME applicant preflighted the airplane and said we were ready to depart. It was early in the morning and it was cool. Dew had formed on the windshield and you couldn't see through it. I asked the applicant how he planned to navigate to the runway. He then said, "Do you want me to clean the windshield?"

A CFI-AME candidate called for taxi clearance. Then he spent a long time completing the Before Taxi checklist. Finally he began to taxi. Students are now taught to slightly lean the mixture during taxi to avoid fouling the spark plugs. This candidate leaned too much. As we left the parking area the right engine failed because of fuel starvation. He restarted the engine and we continued to taxi. On the taxiway the left engine failed because of fuel starvation. The ground controller asked, "Do you really want to go flying today?"

An AME candidate was asked to demonstrate how to handle an engine failure after takeoff. We made a normal takeoff and at 500 feet above the ground the applicant moved the right mixture control lever to the shutoff position. The right engine then stopped running. There we are at 500 feet with the right engine windmilling and no action from the applicant except. "I'm trying to hold blue line!" He was terrified into freeze mode. He could not hear me suggest that he return the right mixture control to the full rich position. I had to take control of the airplane. During the debrief I asked why he hadn't simulated the engine failure by reducing power instead of cutting the mixture. He replied, "No one ever had me fail an engine on takeoff before."

The applicant was five feet tall and weighed 99 pounds. When she demonstrated an engine failure after takeoff she reduced power on the left engine at 500 feet above the ground. Because of her size and leg length she couldn't get full right rudder pedal movement even though her seat was in the full forward position. The airplane began a slow descending left turn with the airspeed decaying through 60 knots. She tried to correct with ailerons. Then we began experiencing a stall buffet. She never thought to restore power on the left engine and get out of danger. I took control and we returned to the airport. During the debrief I suggest that she put a pillow behind her back and the seat so she would be farther forward on the seat and have full rudder authority.

At 4000 feet altitude I asked the CFI-AME applicant to demonstrate an engine shutdown and air start. He feathered the left engine and moved the mixture control for the right engine to the idle cutoff position. Now we were a glider. I asked him, "Why are we losing altitude?"

He replied, "We are descending because we are above single engine service ceiling."

Then I asked, "Why is it so quiet?" No response. "What is wrong with the throttle quadrant?"

He looked and said, "I don't believe I did that."

During a V_{MC} demonstration (See the chapter on aerodynamics for definition of V_{MC}) the applicant let the airplane go too far. The airplane flew through a 90 degree heading change and lost 400 feet. It was quickly getting out of control. The applicant was terrified and pleaded, "Can you help me out!" I took control of the airplane and we returned to the airport. During the debrief I learned that the student had never experienced a true V_{MC} before our flight. During all of his training he had been taught to recover when the stall horn sounded. He was one of many applicants I see that are afraid of this maneuver. Many instructors are afraid of this maneuver. There is a lot of work to do to get the CFIs educated and trained to properly demonstrate the loss of directional control on one engine.

Many airplanes are now equipped with a variety of GPS receivers and flight management systems. It's a real challenge for instructors and examiners to become familiar with all of the systems available. You would think that when a student brings an airplane to the check-ride they would know how to use the installed equipment. I see a lot of applicants that don't know how to use the autopilot and the GPS navigation equipment in the test airplane. Revised PTS procedures are addressing this problem. Examiners have to test the applicant's ability to use all installed equipment. The following check-ride highlights the problem.

The AME candidate was proceeding direct to KHWO from the training area via GPS navigation.

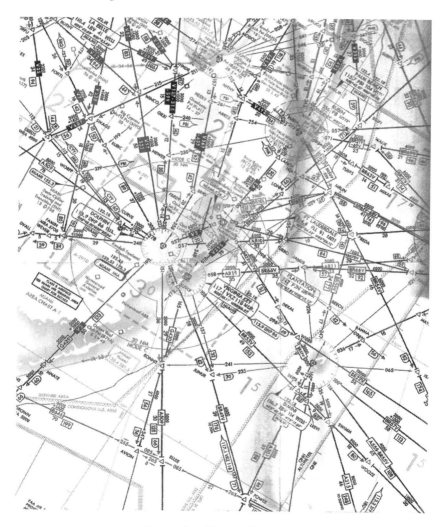

Excerpt from Enroute Chart L-19

Our course would cut through the corner of the Ft. Lauderdale Class C airspace. I asked the applicant to set up the GPS so we could track a 090 course to the airport. (This is done using the OBS mode of the GPS) He had no idea how to set up the GPS. I showed him how to program the GPS to provide the 090 course to the airport. Instead of intercepting and tracking the 090 course the applicant flew parallel about three miles north of the course. Just before I intervened to avoid going into Class C without talking to the Approach Controller, the tower at HWO called us and said, "Do you know where you are?"

We were in the traffic pattern and the tower cleared the AME applicant to land on Runway 9L. The applicant extended his base leg and lined up on final for Runway 9R. There was no other traffic in the pattern so the tower controller was pretty cool. He said, "I guess you're cleared to land on any runway." I advised him that it was a check-ride and that we were done for the day.

A CFI-AME candidate was demonstrating how to make a simulated single engine landing. He said that because it was a single engine landing you should approach a little higher and a little faster than normal. He came over the airport fence at 500 feet above the airport. There was no way we could land on the runway from that position. He said, "I guess I'm a little too high."

The final example in this chapter is a CFI-AME candidate who was demonstrating how to make a simulated single engine landing. On the downwind leg he became uncoordinated. He had too much aileron input which caused the airplane to skid through the air. He let the airplane get dangerously slow and as he turned to final I felt a stall buffet. While all this was going on the applicant was busy reading the Single Engine Landing Checklist and not paying attention to his flying. When I chided him during the debrief about reading in the pattern he became adamant and said, "You must complete the Before Landing Checklist before landing." I responded that he was correct, but the checklist should be done safely and the pilot should not be busy reading a checklist when operating at low level. After all, what is the minimum that you must remember to do before landing? Make sure the landing gear is down and locked.

You're Too Stupid to Be A Pilot

In this chapter I will give you some examples of genuine stupidity so gross that you will wonder not only how did these applicants think they could be pilots but how did they survive childhood. Some examples could get honorable mention in the Darwin Awards competition.

A Commercial Pilot applicant forgot to remove the pitot tube cover during his preflight inspection. The engine was started, taxi clearance received and the aircraft was taxied to the run up pad. After the run up was completed the applicant received a clearance from the tower to, "Taxi into position and Hold." While holding in position on the runway, the applicant was asked the purpose of the red streamer hanging from the pitot tube.

He looked out and said, "I forgot, you hold the brakes and I'll jump out and remove it." For non-pilots the pitot tube cover prevents bugs and dirt from entering the pitot tube. If it is partially blocked by bugs and dirt the airspeed indicator will not work correctly. If the cover is left on it will not work at all. The red streamer is to alert the pilot during the preflight inspection that the cover is still in place.

Picture of a Pitot Tube with Cover

Several CFI-AME (Certified Flight Instructor-Airplane Multiengine) candidates have made this foul up. At a certain busy airport the ground crew at the FBO protects aircraft on the tie down line with large high visibility yellow rubber traffic cones. They usually place one at each wing tip and one at the nose of the aircraft.

Now enter Mr. Stupid. The applicant completes the preflight and enters the aircraft. Engines are started and taxi clearance is requested. The only problem is that the large yellow rubber cone is still in front of the aircraft nose. All of this after I have asked the applicant prior to my boarding the aircraft if the preflight is completed and the aircraft is ready to be moved. I just shake my head in disbelief. One of the more memorable failures caused me terminal eye rolling. The applicant completed the preflight and prepared to board the aircraft. I asked if he had finished his preflight inspection. He said yes. The infernal yellow cone was still in front of the aircraft nose. I asked him if the aircraft was clear to taxi. He said yes. Then I asked him if he had completed a final walk around. Now he became worried and said he would do a final walk around. He walked between the nose of the aircraft and the yellow cone without seeing the cone that was only two feet in front of the aircraft. He finished the walk around and pronounced that the aircraft was ready. As the applicant began to board the airplane I informed him we would not be flying that day and that he should look in front of the aircraft. He just lowered his head and said, "How could I have been so stupid?"

A Private Pilot applicant announced that the windshield was dirty and needed to be cleaned prior to flight. A trip to the supply locker produced some plexiglass cleaner and paper towels. The applicant did a great job of cleaning the outside of the windshield and then said the preflight was complete and prepared to start the engine. The problem was that all of the windshield contamination was on the inside of the windshield and was still restricting vision through it.

A CFI-ASE (Certified Flight Instructor-Airplane Single Engine) applicant forgot to remove the nosewheel chocks during preflight. After engine start he received taxi clearance and attempted to move the aircraft. Of course it wouldn't move because of the chocks. Instead of thinking about what could be wrong, he announced that the aircraft had sunk into the hot asphalt and quickly went to full power. The aircraft immediately jumped over the chocks much to his surprise.

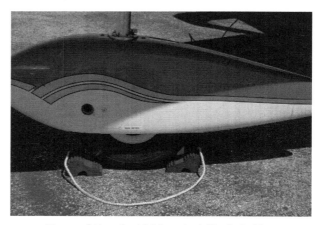

Picture of Aircraft with Nosewheel Chocks in Place

Just when you think it's safe to go to the airport something like this happens. For non-pilots, airplanes with retractable landing gear are protected from accidental gear retraction while the airplane is on the ground by an electrical switch called a squat switch or sometimes called an air/ground switch. It is either a micro switch, or a proximity switch attached to one of the landing gear struts in such a way that when the airplane is on the ground the landing gear electrical circuit is not complete and the landing gear motor cannot be energized. The applicant for CFI-AME finished his preflight and we climbed into the airplane. He turned on the master electrical switch energizing the airplane's electrical system. Then I saw him reach out and move the landing gear selector switch to the "UP" position. I quickly turned off the master switch and asked him what he was thinking. He said, "I am testing the squat switch." I returned the landing gear selector to the "DOWN" position and breathed a sigh of relief. The applicant then said, "Does that mean I fail?"

A CFI-ASE applicant performed a truly mind boggling demonstration after takeoff. During his upwind to crosswind turn he reduced engine manifold pressure to climb setting and began adjusting the engine RPM to climb setting. I noticed that the engine was beginning to run a little rough. A quick check of the aircraft showed me what was wrong. The applicant was reducing the engine RPM by reducing the fuel flow with the mixture control instead of using the propeller governor control. I asked him why the engine was beginning to run rough and his reply was that the engine must be experiencing carburetor icing. I then asked him why he was reducing fuel flow with the mixture control. He replied that the engine RPM was controlled by the fuel flow setting. I told him I was now flying the airplane and we were returning to the airport. He then said, "I guess I failed."

A CFI was flying one night in a Cessna 172 with a student. When they landed they made an emergency telephone call to the school's mechanic telling him that the ailerons had locked up and the student had lost control of the airplane. The CFI had to fly the airplane back to the airport and had just been able to control the airplane using superman force to operate the ailerons. When they looked at the airplane after landing they noticed that both ailerons had been, bent at the tips due to the excessive force needed to operate them. The mechanic got out of bed and drove to the airport. He found that the autopilot was still engaged and that the bent ailerons were the normal twist in the ailerons at their outer ends so they would match the twist in the outer portion of the wings as designed by Cessna.

Picture Showing twist in Cessna 172 Ailerons

A Private Pilot wanted to add an Airplane Multiengine Land rating to his certificate. We completed the oral portion of the practical test and went to the airplane. After completing the upper air work maneuvers I asked the applicant to proceed to Pompano Beach Airpark (KPMP) to conduct the pattern work. As we proceeded toward Pompano I noticed that the applicant was having trouble remembering the ATIS (Air Traffic Information Service which gives the airport weather, runway in use etc.) frequency. I suggested that he consult the Miami Sectional Chart to determine the frequency. The applicant said he had not brought the chart with him. I asked him what he planned to use for navigation information and he replied, "All I need to know is in the computer." The test was being conducted in a Diamond Aircraft TwinStar (DA-42) and the Garmin 1,000 flight system in the airplane contains a wealth of navigation information available to the pilot. Unfortunately, after five minutes the applicant was still trying to access the Garmin 1,000 to find the frequency. I told him the frequency and we continued the flight test to Pompano Beach Airport where the applicant had a problem handling the airplane after takeoff with a simulated engine failure. He allowed the aircraft to become dangerously slow when climbing out after a simulated engine failure. After I issued him a Notice of Disapproval I ragged him pretty good about flying without a navigation chart. A few days later he returned for a retest. We reviewed what procedures to follow in the event of an engine failure after liftoff and went to the airplane. After the engines were started I asked him if he had brought his Miami Sectional with him. He said, "I don't have one." I then asked him why he had not brought the chart. He said that during the previous night a thief had broken into his car and had taken his flight bag and the chart had been in the flight bag. I asked him why he had not stopped at the airport pilot shop to purchase a new Sectional Chart for the flight test. He said, "I didn't have time."

Picture of a DA-42

During a Private Pilot Airplane Single Engine Land (PVT-ASEL) test the applicant showed me his weight and balance calculations for our flight. I noticed that his calculated takeoff weight was 30 pounds heavier than the allowable maximum takeoff weight per the aircraft flight manual. I asked him if there was a problem with the weight and balance of the aircraft for our flight. He said he didn't think there was a problem I asked him to explain why he planned to takeoff 30 pounds overweight. He said, "No problem. My instructor and I do it all the time." Egads! What was that instructor thinking? I had a few choice words for him when I called about the student's failure.

A Commercial Pilot Airplane Multiengine Land (COM-AMEL) applicant gave me quite a thrill shortly after takeoff in a Beechcraft Baron (BE-55). At 100 feet above the runway I observed him to lean forward and reach down near the left fuel valve selector handle. Shortly thereafter the left engine began to fail. I noticed that the fuel selector had been placed in the off position. Although the engine was not running the propeller was still wind milling. The applicant had no idea that the engine had failed and continued to climb away from the airport. The airplane began slowing and the climb performance was deteriorating. I asked the applicant if he thought anything might be wrong. He said, "Nothing is wrong, sir." Then I asked him why our performance was so poor. He said, "I need more power, sir." Then I took control of the aircraft.

Turning the fuel selector back to the on position restored fuel flow and the engine came back to life. During the debrief I asked why he had shutoff the fuel. He said that he thought he had left the fuel selector in the crossfeed position after he had done his ground checks and knew that it must be in the on position for takeoff so when he remembered he reached down and changed it. He didn't think he had mistakenly selected the off position. When I asked him to then explain why the left engine had failed he said, "I must have shut off the fuel." He had no coherent answer to my question that if he thought the selector was in crossfeed why had he done the takeoff at all? The next day an instructor at the school reported to me that the applicant was telling people that I had tricked him by turning off the fuel to the left engine when he wasn't looking. When we met for the retest I asked him if he remembered our preflight briefing from the previous attempt wherein I had advised him that in the air I would simulate an engine failure by retarding a throttle and in no case would I give him an engine out emergency below 500 feet above the ground. "I remember, sir." I told him the same procedures would be followed on the retest. I then told him he should correct comments he made earlier about who had accidentally shut off the fuel on his previous check-ride.

Picture of a BE-55

A COM-AMEL applicant was briefed that during the flight portion of the test I would simulate an emergency that would require the applicant to fully shut down an engine in flight and then accomplish an air start. I cautioned him that when shutting down the engine that he should be careful to identify the correct throttle, propeller and mixture control levers before moving them so that the operating engine was not accidentally shut down. I told him about a commuter turboprop airplane that had an engine failure shortly after take off and that the crew had misidentified the failed engine and mistakenly shut down the good engine resulting in a water landing in the Pacific Ocean just outside the breakers. He laughed and said, "How could anyone be so stupid?" We went to the airplane, and took off. While we were approximately 4000 feet above the ground (4000AGL) I said, "Captain, the right engine is on fire!" The applicant closed the right throttle, feathered the right propeller and closed the mixture for the left engine. Now we have the left engine wind milling and the right engine with a feathered propeller resulting in no power being produced by either engine. It was very quiet. The airplane began to descend.

At 3500 AGL I asked the applicant, "Why is it so quiet?"

He said, "It's because we have an engine out." I asked him why we couldn't maintain altitude. He said, "We need more power from the left engine." Then he pushed the left throttle to full power.

At 3300 AGL I directed his attention to the left mixture control and then I advanced it to full fuel flow. The left engine immediately began running at full power and the descent was arrested. Then I restarted the right engine and told the applicant to return to the airport. The applicant said, "I can't believe that I was so stupid."

Applicant emergency engine shutdowns always elevate my adrenalin flow. You would be amazed how frequently the applicants shut down both engines by mistake. On another COM-AMEL check-ride I said the left engine was on fire. The applicant closed the left throttle, feathered the left engine and moved the right engine mixture control lever to cutoff. Now both engines are shutdown. About five seconds later I asked the applicant, "Don't you think it's kind of quiet?"

He replied, "Of course it is. I just shut down an engine." This was another flight test where I had to restore power on one with the mixture and then restart the other engine.

Even instructor applicants are not immune to this kind of failure. On a CFI-AME check-ride I simulated a left engine fire. The applicant quickly closed the left throttle, moved the left propeller control to feather, and moved the right engine mixture control to cutoff. Then he said, "I can't believe that I just failed myself!"

There is another popular way to mishandle an engine emergency. Select the wrong magnetos to turn off.

For non-pilots, magnetos supply the electrical power to the engine's sparkplugs. A piston aircraft engine has two spark plugs per cylinder for safety and to insure complete combustion of the air-fuel mixture in the cylinder. There are two magnetos for the engine, each supplying electrical power to a set of spark plugs. They are commonly called, "Left and right mag." A magneto is a simple device. A magnet rotates inside a coil of wire thus producing electricity. The electricity is stored in a capacitor until a set of points (sounds like your car, eh?) activates and allows the stored electrical energy to go down the wiring harness to the correct spark plug. The magnetos are driven by the engine, so as long as the engine is turning the magnetos will produce electricity and power the spark plugs. Before takeoff the magnetos are checked to be sure each is functioning properly. The engine power is advanced to a mid-range power setting and the right magneto is turned off. As only the left magneto is operating the engine rpm will slightly decrease. Then the right magneto is turned back on and the left magneto is turned off to check the right magneto. After the test is completed both magnetos are turned on. A twin-engine airplane will have four magnetos, two per engine.

Now enter Captain Stupid. The flight test was in a Piper Seminole (PA-44) twin-engine airplane. The COM-AMEL applicant was told that the right engine oil pressure had just dropped to zero and that oil was spewing from the engine cowling. The applicant said, "Do you want me to shut down the engine?' I told him this was one of the simulated emergencies that we had discussed during the oral portion of his test and that he should shut down the engine. He successfully pulled the throttle, propeller and mixture levers for the right engine Then he proceeded to accomplish the Engine Secure checklist. The design of the PA-44 engine controls has the magneto on/off switches built as rocker switches and they are located in pairs on a side panel left of the pilot. With one finger you can simultaneously turn off both left and right magnetos for the engine. The applicant reached over and in error simultaneously turned off both magnetos for the left engine. Another quiet time in the airplane. This error is so prevalent that one of the local flight schools won't let their students actually move the magneto switches. Their students are trained to only touch the switches and announce that they have turned them off. So now they can fail by inappropriate touching?

PA-44 Side Panel Showing Magneto Switches

Another CFI-AME applicant demonstrated an interesting variation of this. On his check-ride in a PA-44, he successfully completed the throttle, propeller and mixture moves for engine shutdown and then continued with the Engine Secure checklist. He turned off the left engine left magneto and the right engine left magneto. I asked him to explain what he had done. He said, "I turned off the mags for the left engine." I was speechless. Here was an instructor applicant that didn't know each engine has a left and right magneto.

There also are problems with magnetos on engine air starts. On a multiengine check-ride, after an engine has been shutdown and some single engine maneuvering has been accomplished, the engine must be restarted in the air. The aircraft manufacturers provide a checklist for the restart.

A COM-AMEL applicant had successfully completed a left engine shutdown in a Piper Seneca (PA-34) and was working his way through the air start checklist. He forgot to turn the magnetos on. He activated the engine starter and managed to get the propeller out of feather. The engine was rotating at 1500 rpm, which was enough to show some fuel flow on the left engine fuel flow gauge. After five minutes I asked him why it was taking so long to see a temperature rise on the left engine cylinder head temperature gauge (CHT). He said, "I need more power." I let him advance the left throttle to full open. There was no temperature rise. I suggested that he review the air start checklist. He read the checklist and said that everything had been done. I asked what he thought about the engine rpm oscillating between 1400 and 1600 rpm when it should be about 2500 rpm. It was a big mystery to him. At this point I had to takeover the flight. If he turned the magnetos on with the throttle full open and the mixture full rich, there was a great risk of an engine backfire as the cylinders would be full of fuel when the spark plugs fired. This could lead to damage of the intake and exhaust manifolds or even cylinder damage from detonation.

Picture of PA-34

Another COM-AMEL applicant was using a Beechcraft Duchess (BE-76) for his check-ride. Many BE-76 airplanes have propellers equipped with unfeathering accumulators. The accumulator stores hydraulic energy that is used to bring the propeller out of the feather position during an air start. It is a much smoother start than using the engine starter to rotate the engine until the propeller begins to unfeather. As soon as you move the propeller control from feather to high rpm the accumulator begins to unfeather the propeller and the engine begins to rotate. After an uneventful shutdown of the right engine the applicant attempted an air start. The applicant overlooked the checklist item that called for him to turn the magnetos on before unfeathering the propeller. Now we have the right engine controls set as follows: throttle open about ½ inch, propeller lever full rpm and the mixture full rich. The unfeathering accumulator did its job so the propeller was out of feather and rotating around 2300 rpm, which is in the normal operating range. But with no spark the engine is not running. The applicant saw the rpms were at 2300 and thought the engine was running. I waited about two minutes and asked him why the right engine CHT was so low. He said, "I need to advance the throttle to get more power." He did that and then I asked him why we hadn't accelerated to a normal cruise speed. He finally saw that the magnetos for the right engine were off. Before he could touch the magneto switch I told him, "Do not touch the mags under penalty of death!" The right engine was full of fuel and if he turned the mags on there could be a destructive backfire. I retarded the throttle to idle and pulled the mixture lever to cutoff and waited a couple of minutes before turning the right engine magnetos on. Then I advanced the mixture lever full forward to start the engine. Then I advanced the throttle to an engine warm-up power setting. The applicant said, "I guess I didn't pass."

Picture of a BE-76

A final example of a botched engine air start involved not seeing what you are looking at. The applicant had done an engine shutdown without incident and was following the air start checklist. When he read the item "Avionics Switch OFF" he misunderstood it to be "Master Switch OFF." He turned off the master switch, which killed electrical power to the entire airplane. No battery power, no alternator power, no lights, no avionics, no intercom, no starters, you get the idea. Remember the explanation of magnetos? The operating engine continued to run as the magnetos are not connected to the airplane electrical system. The applicant repeatedly pushed on the engine start switch but nothing happened. After three or four minutes of this the applicant told me that, "The engine starter has failed." I told him that I could not hear him over the intercom. He talked louder. I asked him why all of the avionics were not working. We couldn't see any of the communicatio n or navigation frequencies and the GPS moving map page was only black. He said, "All of my attempts to start the engine with a bad starter must have depleted the battery." I finally told him that he had mistakenly turned the battery off and that if he turned it on we could then start the engine.

An applicant for Airline Transport Pilot AMEL was preparing to fly the LOC-RWY 15 at Pompano Beach Airpark (KPMP). The applicant was flying as a copilot for an airline and had over 400 hours of instrument experience recorded in his logbook. He listened to the Airport Traffic Information Service (ATIS) for the current weather and other pertinent information such as the runway in use. He noted that the runway in use was Runway 24.

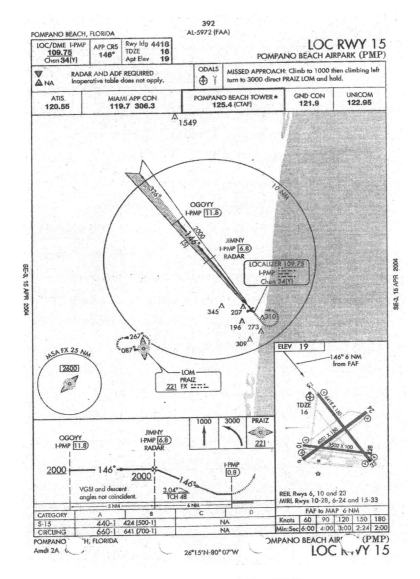

LOC-RWY 15 Approach Plate KPMP

He briefed the approach and said that the Minimum Descent Altitude would be 440'. Very interesting as the circling approach minimum is 660 and we would be circling to land on Runway 24. He passed by the final approach fix (JIMNY) and flew two miles at 2000 before he decided to begin his descent. During the approach he allowed the course deviation indicator (CDI) to reach full scale deflection to the left, corrected and then went full scale deflection to the right. (The ATP test standard is no more than 1/4 scale deflection at any time after passing the final approach fix). At 500 I asked him, "When do you plan to stop your descent?" He was clueless regarding the circling minimums and also had forgotten to time the approach. When I inquired about his poor performance on the approach he said, "The airliners have autopilots to help out and on this airplane I have to do everything."

The next example has been promoted from the chapter regarding Instrument Airplane check-rides to this chapter. After reviewing it you will see why. The applicant for Instrument Airplane was being vectored by Air Traffic Control (ATC) for the NDB-RWY 8 approach at Ft. Lauderdale Executive Airport (KFXE). This approach has since been retired and replaced with a GPS approach.

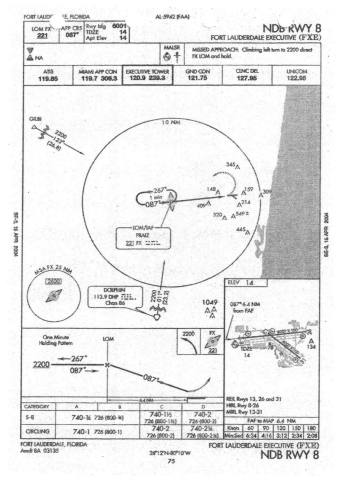

Approach Plate for NDB-RWY 8 at KFXE

The applicant tuned in the NDB frequency 221 for FX. He forgot to listen to the Morse Code identifier for the NDB to determine if it was suitable for navigation. He also tuned the Number 1 VOR receiver to the Dolphin VOR (DHP) and set the Omnidirectional Bearing Selector (OBS) to radial 011, which would provide a backup to the NDB needle reversal to determine when he was crossing FX. For non-pilots, the NDB indicator needle arrowhead always points to the station. When you are inbound it points forward and when you cross over the station it reverses and points to the rear.

Picture of a NDB Course Indicator

The applicant failed to notice that the NDB indicator needle was rotating like a second hand on a clock. It was obvious that the NDB transmitter was not working or the NDB radio in the airplane had failed. If the applicant had remembered to listen for the NDB identifier he might have caught that fact. But he didn't listen and he continued to fly the approach oblivious to the rotating navigation needle. The Approach Controller told him to, "Fly heading 120 and intercept the final course inbound. Maintain two thousand two hundred until Praiz." The applicant flew through the inbound course about two miles west of FX and continued on the 120-degree heading. When the DHP indicator needle showed crossing the 011 radial he began to descend on the 120-degree heading. At that time we were about one mile south of FX. After a mile or so past FX, I had to intervene so as to avoid going into the Class C airspace at Ft. Lauderdale International Airport (KFLL). I asked the applicant what he was using for course guidance. He replied, "I thought the controller gave me a vector to the airport."

An applicant for Private Pilot ASEL never got past the logbook review. I noticed that his long cross country flight (150 nm minimum total distance, landings at three airports and with one leg at least 50 nm) was from Ft.

Lauderdale Executive Airport (KFXE) to Naples Airport (KAPF) to Pompano Beach Airpark (KPMP) then returning to KFXE. His flight time for this trip was logged as 3.6 hours. I know that this trip should have taken about 2 hours in the airplane that he used. I asked what took so long. He replied that he had flown from KFXE to KAPF and back to KFXE. He realized that he needed more solo cross country time to meet the Private Pilot cross country flight experience requirements so he did a touch and go at KFXE and then flew to the local practice area. He circled around in the practice area for about an hour and then remembered that he had to go to three airports on his long cross-country trip so he did a touch and go at KPMP before returning to KFXE. There could be no check-ride that day as the applicant did not meet the minimum experience requirements. I had a very interesting conversation with the instructor who approved this cross country trip.

Then there was the CFI who made a logbook entry per TSA regulations that he had verified through a US Passport that the student was a citizen of the United States. The only problem was that the student was a French citizen as evidenced by his French Passport that he showed me as proof of citizenship.

Now I would like to present my three nominees for the Most Stupid Pilot Award.

An applicant for Certified Flight Instructor-Instrument Airplane (CFI-IA) repeatedly cancelled his check-ride because he couldn't pass the written examination. Finally his instructor called me and said the applicant had now passed the written test and scheduled the check-ride. On the day of the test I reviewed the written test results and found that the applicant had passed the written test on his fourth attempt. Unfortunately the applicant had tried four times to pass the Instrument Rating Airplane (IRA) written examination instead of the Flight Instructor Instrument (FII) written examination that was required for the CFI-IA test. What is even more amazing is that the applicant had to have passed the IRA sometime in the past in order to get his Instrument Airplane rating on his Commercial Pilot certificate!

An applicant for Airline Transport Pilot (ATP) flew into Ft. Lauderdale, FL the night before his scheduled check-ride. When he packed for the trip he had placed his pilot logbook, written test score, commercial pilot certificate, airman medical certificate and his check-ride application form (Form 8710) in his luggage. You have guessed correctly. The airline lost his luggage. There was no check-ride that day. The FAA could confirm the written test score, commercial pilot certificate and medical certificate by a fax message. A new 8710 could be prepared. But without the logbook or other records to verify that the applicant met the experience requirements for ATP I could not proceed with the check-ride.

A CFI-AME check-ride was completed. The applicant had done well and I prepared his temporary CFI-AME certificate. I gave it to him and he reviewed it carefully. Then he pulled out his temporary commercial pilot certificate that had recently been issued by another examiner and said, "I won't be needing this anymore." He walked over to a paper-shredding machine and ran his temporary commercial pilot certificate through the shredder. I asked him if he had noticed the limitation on his new CFI certificate that said it was only valid when accompanied by his commercial pilot certificate. "Holy #&$%!!! How could I have been so stupid?" He exclaimed. He opened the shredding machine and retrieved a large amount of shredded paper. Then he began an attempt to solve the puzzle. He tried to find matching strips of paper and tape them together in an attempt to restore the shredded temporary certificate. I calmed him down and told him to call the other examiner, confess his stupidity, and ask for a replacement temporary commercial pilot certificate.

This brings us to end to this chapter. As you read through this book you may think a lot of other pilots were just as stupid and made equally dumb mistakes and should have been included here, but I thought that these were especially noteworthy. Oh yes, of the above three nominees I vote for Exhibit Number One.

Assorted Atrocities

After I had completed the other chapters detailing check-rides by types I noticed that I had a big stack of notes left over. This chapter is a compendium of many different types of check-rides that were memorable each in their own way.

Oral Exams

Once in a while I have a very frustrating oral examination experience. Some students always answer a question by first repeating the original question. It goes like this:

Me:	"Explain the airplane's fuel system"
Student:	"Explain the airplane's fuel system. It has two fuel tanks etc."
Me:	"What is the relationship between lift and drag?"
Student:	"What is the relationship between lift and drag? Drag is the byproduct etc."
Me:	"How do you determine takeoff distance to clear a 50 foot obstacle?"
Student:	"How do you determine takeoff distance to clear a 50 foot obstacle?"

You get the idea. Two hours of this monkey-see monkey-do questions and answers. I guess that some people must first restate the question to themselves before they can think about the answer.

Sometimes the applicant has a lot of books and notes for reference. I get to watch the top of their heads as they read answers from their reference materials, never providing an answer from their mind. After two or three answers like this I ask them to put away their books and tell me what they know. Amazing to most applicants, they can provide the information without using the books.

A candidate for CFI-IA failed his oral examination. He had almost no knowledge regarding CFI-IA privileges and limitations and was unable to explain information on en route charts and approach plates, ATC procedures or the Practical Test Standards (PTS) for Instrument Airplane. He didn't have the Instrument Airplane PTS in his possession and admitted to not having read FAR Part 91, Instrument Flight Rules, or the Aeronautical Information Manual Chapter Five, ATC Procedures. He made bad jokes in attempt to cover up his lack of knowledge. I had a long talk with the recommending instructor about this applicant.

When reviewing the logbook for a CFI-AME candidate it was determined that the applicant had 14.4 hours of Pilot in Command (PIC) time in multiengine airplanes. I asked the applicant what was the PIC requirement for this check-ride. He answered, "It is 15.0 hours. We figured that the check-ride would take about 1.5 hours so I would have enough to qualify." At least he knew that he would be PIC on his check-ride. Unfortunately for him, you must have 15.0 hours to qualify to start the check-ride. Another call made to an unhappy recommending instructor.

A Private Pilot AMEL applicant forgot to bring his medical certificate with him when he came for his check-ride. He asked, "Could I use a copy from the school's file?"

Another applicant had failed his oral examination. As I was preparing the Disapproval Notice (Pink Slip) he said, "Could you not turn in the failure notice? I will pay you for the retest but show it as a test. My father will pull me out of flight school if I have a failure." I felt badly for this applicant but I had to process the file. I talked with his father and convinced him that many pilots have had a failed check-ride in their career and this failure might be just the incentive needed for his son to really apply himself and not have another failure in his training program. His father agreed and his son did a fine job on the retest and subsequent check-rides.

Candidates for You're Too Stupid to be a Pilot

A CFI-ASE applicant forgot to bring his Miami Sectional Chart with him for the flight portion of his test. He tried to convince me that it was okay to fly without a chart if you knew the area. Unfortunately for him, when he tried to return to Pompano Beach Airpark (KPMP) he became lost. I let him work about 10 minutes, but he could not locate himself and I had to give him a heading to the airport.

During the certificate review portion of a Commercial Pilot AMEL check-ride I noticed that the applicant's medical certificate said, "Corrective lenses required." I saw that the applicant was wearing black horn rimmed spectacles. When we started the flying portion of the test I saw that he was wearing sunglasses and assumed that they were prescription lenses. When the applicant put on view restricting foggles for the instrument approach portion of his test he wore no glasses. I then thought that he must have put on contact lenses before we went to the airplane and that the sunglasses were not prescription lenses. After we parked the airplane at the conclusion of the flight test, I asked the applicant when had he put on his contact lenses. He said he wasn't wearing contact lenses.

I then asked, "Where are your glasses?"

He replied, "They're in the back," as he pointed to his flight bag on the rear seat.

I asked to see his medical certificate and said, "What does it say on your medical?"

He looked at his medical certificate and said, "I can see good enough."

I then said, "Apparently your Flight Surgeon didn't think so." I told him he was lucky that I was a Designated Examiner not a FAA Inspector because I was issuing a Disapproval Notice but the Inspector could issue a violation.

I heard this on the Pompano Beach Airpark (KPMP) tower frequency. I have left out the complete aircraft call sign to protect the pilot's identity. The aircraft was based at KPMP.

The pilot said, "Pompano Tower, this is Cirrus xxxCD. My screens are out and I don't know where I am. Can you help me?"

What the pilot is talking about is that the two screens that provide flight instrumentation and engine and navigation information including a moving map display have failed and there is nothing appearing on either screen. Cirrus aircraft also have backup flight instruments and two Garmin 430 GPS navigation radios that are sufficient to fly the aircraft if this should happen.

Tower said, "Cirrus xxxCD, ident."

The tower has asked the pilot to activate the identification feature of the airplane's transponder.

The pilot said, "Identing"

Tower "It looks like you're lined up with Runway 13 at Executive Airport. Turn left to a suggested heading of 060 and that will put you on a right base for Runway 15."

Egads! This pilot was lining up with Runway 13 at Ft. Lauderdale Executive Airport (KFXE) and was within 5 miles of KPMP. He was within sight of KPMP. If he couldn't see it he still had the two Garmin 430s to navigate with. He is very typical of some of the new pilots that are totally lost without their moving map displays. Whatever happened to pilotage and dead reckoning?

A Private Pilot ASEL couldn't understand why his cross-country flight planning calculations for time en route and fuel consumption were so far off. He had used the side of his plotter that was scaled for World Aeronautical Charts, which are 1:1,000,000 instead of the Sectional Charts which are 1:500,000.

A Commercial Pilot ASEL had just finished performing a steep spiral descent and was at an altitude of 1000 feet above ground. I requested that the next maneuver be 8's on Pylons. The applicant climbed to 2000 feet above ground and began the maneuver.

I asked him, "Why was are you so high?"

He replied, "I may have to adjust for my speed."

I asked him, "What is your pivotal altitude?" (Pivitol Altitude is the altitude where the aircraft appears to pivot about a point instead of turning about a point. That is the altitude where the 8's on Pylons maneuver is performed.)

He said, "760 feet."

I said, "How do you know that?"

He replied, "That's what my instructor told me."

I asked, "How can you calculate the pivotal altitude?" He had no idea how to do it. It is an easy formula: (Ground Speed)^2 divided by 11.3.

A Private Pilot AMEL was asked to fly the ILS-8 approach at Ft. Lauderdale Executive Airport (KFXE). As we approached the airport it became obvious that he had no approach charts in the airplane. I asked him what were his intentions and he said, "I don't need the approach plate because I have the approach memorized."

So I asked him, "What is the glide-slope crossing altitude?"

He replied, "I don't know."

I asked, "Where is the Missed Approach Point?"

He said, "I don't know."

I asked him, "If the glide-slope fails and we have to do the Localizer Approach, what would be the flight time for the approach?"

Again, "I don't know."

Well, three strikes and you're out at the old ball game. What are people thinking? Are they really flying like this?

An applicant for COM-ASEL showed up for his check-ride at 800 a.m. He said he had worked Line Service all night at the local FBO and was too tired for the test. You would think he would have known he would be tired after working all night and would have scheduled the check-ride for another day and time. At least he knew not to fly when tired.

Before Takeoff

An applicant for ATP-AMEL performed a check of the engine magnetos in this fashion. For each engine he shut off both left and right magnetos simultaneously. Each engine's rpm dropped to about 1500 at which time he turned both magnetos back on simultaneously. When he had completed this procedure for both engines he announced, "Mag checks ok." In his defense, he had not flown a piston powered airplane for ten years. But don't you think someone preparing for a flight test would learn the correct procedures for his airplane?

A PVT-AMEL applicant flying a Beechcraft Duchess (BE-76) said that he had completed his Before Takeoff Checklist and called the tower for takeoff clearance. The problem was that after he had checked the wing flap operation he had forgotten to retract the flaps to their takeoff position, which is the UP position. He would be taking off with the flaps in the full down position, which is the landing position. As we taxied onto the runway I called the tower to cancel the takeoff and requested clearance back to the parking ramp. The applicant had no idea what was wrong and said, "Did I fail?"

A candidate for CFI-AME never made it to the airplane having failed the oral examination phase of his check-ride. Among other problems during the oral, he carefully showed me how to calculate the distance required to clear a 50-foot obstacle on takeoff using the Rate of Climb Chart instead of the Takeoff Distance Chart.

Takeoff

An applicant for Private Pilot AMEL was asked to perform a short field takeoff. His first error was forgetting to turn on the fuel boost pumps as specified by the checklist. He accelerated down the runway past 70 knots airspeed which is the rotation speed specified in the Pilot's Operating Handbook for short field takeoffs. We reached 85 knots airspeed and the applicant was using significant elevator force to keep the airplane on the ground with no indication that he was about to rotate the airplane. At this point we had about 150 of runway remaining. I had to take control of the airplane, lifted off the runway and established a climb.

The applicant said, "I was trying to reach blue line." He had the mistaken idea that you don't rotate until you reach the single engine best rate of climb speed (V_{YSE}). He also confirmed that he had not been aware that we were about to run off the end of the runway.

Navigation

During a PVT-ASEL check-ride in an aircraft equipped with a Garmin 1000 flight management system I asked the applicant to select the VOR mode on the Heading Situation Indicator (HSI). This is done by pressing on a bezel key at the bottom of the Pilot Flight Display (PFD). In the GPS mode the course indicator is magenta and in the VOR mode it is green. The applicant was unable to make the VOR selection. He said that his instructor never showed him how to do it and had told him to always use the GPS for navigation. You would at first think the instructor had failed to do his duty. I checked into this. The school has an approved Part 141 course and the syllabus includes training for the use of the HSI. If the instructor had followed the lesson plans the student would have had the training. The student training records showed he had been given the training by the instructor. So was this was another case of the student blaming his forgetfulness and poor performance on his instructor?

A PVT-ASEL applicant departed Belle Glade Airport (X10) for Pompano Beach Airpark (KPMP). He followed the wrong canal and began to fly toward Palm Beach International Airport (KPBI). When we were 11 miles from Palm Beach I asked him what city was dead ahead. He said it was Pompano Beach.

There he was, 20 miles off course with no clue about his position. He never thought to check his position with his VOR or DME as he flew from X10.

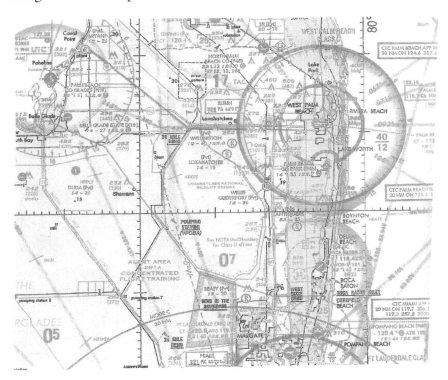

Excerpt from Miami Sectional Chart
Showing X10), PBI and PMP

An applicant for COM-AMEL took off from Runway 33 at Lantana Airport (KLNA) and began to fly west toward the practice area at an altitude of 1000 feet. If you look at the above illustration you can see that the inner circle of the Palm Beach Class C Airspace, which begins at the surface has a cutout for the KLNA traffic pattern. As we headed west the applicant penetrated the Class C airspace northwest of KLNA. I said to the student, "Look at your GPS map. You are in Class C without a clearance."

He replied, "We do it all the time." He was incredulous that he was failed for this error.

A candidate for PVT-ASEL completed turns about a point near the Boca Racetrack west of the Boca Raton Airport (KBCT). I said, "Let's go to Lantana and do a short field approach and landing." The candidate climbed from 1000 feet up to 1800 feet. I knew that we were approaching the Palm Beach Class C Airspace. So I said, "What altitude do you intend to fly to Lantana?"

He said, "Fifteen hundred." and descended to 1500 feet and continued toward Lantana Airport (KLNA).

I asked him, "Why is the message light on the GPS receiver blinking." He checked and read the message that we were approaching the Palm Beach Class C airspace. He continued on. I suggested that he review his Miami Sectional Chart. He looked it over and said we were on course for Lantana Airport. Then I changed the GPS presentation to the moving map mode and asked him what the concentric rings around West Palm Beach Airport (KPBI) indicated. Since he had not contacted Palm Beach Approach for permission to enter the Class C airspace, I told him that he had to immediately descend below 1200 feet and exit the Class C airspace.

Then he said, "I guess I messed up." That's for sure. If an examiner asks you what you are doing, you better look around to see what might be going astray.

A PVT-ASEL applicant called the Pompano Tower for landing clearance and reported overhead the, "Bend in the Sawgrass." This is where the Sawgrass Expressway makes a 90-degree turn from west to south and pilots use this spot as a reporting point for both Pompano Tower and Ft. Lauderdale Executive Tower. The problem was that the applicant was several miles east of this spot and was inside the Class D airspace of Boca Raton Airport (KBCT) without talking to BCT Tower. He had no idea of his current position.

Flight Maneuvers

A Private Pilot ASEL candidate was performing a power off stall. At the point of the stall the airplane began to turn left. He applied full right aileron but made no rudder control input. He wondered why I failed him for his technique.

Another Private Pilot ASEL candidate was less lucky. He too was doing a power off stall and as the airplane stalled it began to turn left. This applicant simultaneously applied full power and full left rudder. The airplane made a nice snap entry into a left spin. He cried out at the top of his voice, "Please help me!"

We had plenty of altitude so I told him to reduce the power to idle, neutralize the ailerons and apply full right rudder. When the spin stopped I told him to push forward to break the stall and when we were flying again to level off. Then I told him to return to the airport. That was enough excitement for the day.

We were flying over Interstate 75 about two miles west of a VFR reporting point called the Andytown Tollgate when I asked a Commercial Pilot ASEL candidate to perform 8's on Pylons. Most applicants would select pylons along Interstate 75 such as crossovers or bridges. This applicant decided to fly about six miles east ending up overhead the town of Weston. He selected two swimming pools as his pylons and descended to 850 feet above the ground, which he said was the pivotal altitude for us and began the maneuver. I asked him what the Federal Air Regulations (FARs) said about minimum altitude above populated areas. (The correct answer is 1000 feet except for taking off and landing.) He said, "Fifteen hundred feet."

I then asked, "So why are we maneuvering over the houses at 850 feet?" He answered, "Does this mean I fail?"

A Private Pilot ASEL applicant was flying at 1500 feet when I requested that he perform a maneuver called Turn About a Point. This maneuver consists of two complete circles of constant radius, constant altitude and constant airspeed around a point on the ground. The Practical Test Standard (PTS) states that the maneuver should be performed at a selected altitude between 600 and 1000 feet above the ground. This applicant climbed from 1500 feet to 2000 feet so I questioned him about why he had climbed.

Me: "What altitude are you planning to do the maneuver?"
Him: "Two thousand feet."
Me: "Why two thousand feet?"
Him: "That's what we do at Embry Riddle."
Me: "Are you flying at Embry Riddle or are you doing a Private check-ride?"
Him: "A check-ride,"
Me: "What does the PTS say about ground reference maneuver altitude?"
Him: "I don't know."
Me: "It says 600 to 1000 feet above the ground."
Him: "Oh."

Then he proceeded to perform the maneuver at 2000 feet. I shook my head in disbelief. How could anyone disregard such a direct hint?

Approach and Landing

A Private Pilot ASEL applicant was returning to Pompano Beach Airpark. He mistuned the frequency for the tower and couldn't get a response from the tower. Then we heard an airliner report, "Descending from Flight Level 260 to Flight Level 190." The applicant couldn't understand why an airliner would be talking on the tower frequency. Finally, I had to tell him as we were getting close to the airport and had to talk to the tower on the correct frequency.

A Private Pilot ASEL applicant was returning to the airport from the northeast and called the Pompano Tower for landing instructions. The tower controller said, "Report passing the shoreline and enter a left downwind for Runway 10." The applicant entered a left downwind for Runway 15 and opposite the approach end of Runway 15 began a descent. He continued descending in a northwesterly direction until he was 400 feet above the houses. The tower called, "Are you okay?" I called back and said it was a check-ride and asked to maneuver for a landing on Runway 10. The applicant was clueless about his error until the debrief on the ground.

A Commercial Pilot AMEL applicant was preparing to land a Beechcraft Baron (BE-55). He entered the traffic pattern at 140 knots and never slowed the aircraft. This caused him to get dangerously close to a Cessna 172 that was ahead of us in the pattern and he had to abort the landing and perform a go-around. On his second attempt to land he again kept his speed too fast.

This time the tower told him to reduce to his final approach speed for traffic separation, but he didn't hear the tower or see the airplane in front of us in the pattern. He had to make another go-around. On the third attempt he allowed the speed to get too slow and developed a very high sink rate. Self preservation kicked in and I had to intervene and fly the airplane. The applicant said, "Did I do something wrong?"

Instrument Flight

Late model aircraft equipped with GPS receivers, moving maps and flight directors and autopilots are a joy to fly. Unfortunately some pilots get mesmerized by the neat equipment and forget that they are supposed to be controlling an airplane. Here are some examples of forgetting that you are in an airplane:

More often than you would think, a pilot has just taken off and at about 200 feet above the ground puts all of his attention inside the cockpit so he can program his GPS for his route of flight. What happened to programming the trip before taking off? Truly amazing are the pilots who can't find their way from Pompano Beach Airpark (KPMP) to Ft. Lauderdale Executive Airport (KFXE) without entering KFXE into the GPS just after takeoff so they can determine a heading to fly. Egads! You can see KFXE just after liftoff. It's only five miles away.

An applicant for an Instrument Airplane rating was being vectored for an ILS approach and was given a heading of 060 degrees to intercept the localizer. The applicant devoted so much attention trying to program the approach into his GPS receiver that he failed to notice that the course deviation indicator (CDI) had passed through the center and he continued on the 060 heading well north of the localizer until he had full right deflection of the CDI. At this point I had to alert Approach Control that we were on a check-ride and that we would immediately make a course correction.

Another applicant was supposed to be flying the ILS-8R approach at North County Airport (F45). He couldn't understand why the navigation instruments seemed to be giving incorrect indications. He thought he was near the final approach point, but the distance to the airport was showing as 45 miles and the localizer and glide-slope indicators were inactive. I finally had to tell him that he had incorrectly programmed the GPS for the ILS-8 at Ft. Lauderdale Executive Airport (KFXE), and that he had never changed his navigation mode from GPS to VLOC (VOR, or Localizer).

A similar problem happened on a type-rating ride in an Embraer 145 being conducted at San Jose dos Campos, Brazil. This aircraft has the capability to select either VOR or ADF, as the input to the Remote Magnetic Indicator (RMI). The change is made with a selector switch on the glare shield. The applicant was asked to perform an ADF approach but forgot to change the RMI from VOR to ADF. At the conclusion of the approach I told the applicant that he had flown a very nice approach but that we were about five miles from the airport having tracked the course from a nearby VOR instead of the ADF.

Years ago there was a NDB-8 approach at Ft. Lauderdale Executive Airport (KFXE) that has been decommissioned. The applicant for Instrument Airplane was performing this approach. The minimum descent altitude (MDA) was 740 feet. As we descended through 600 feet with no indication of leveling off I asked, "Why are you at 600 feet?"

The applicant replied, "I wasn't paying attention to the altimeter."

I often wonder about things like this. Would he have continued to ground impact if I hadn't said something?

An applicant for CFI-IA (Instrument Airplane) who had failed his first attempt had to accomplish an ILS approach on a retest. Our plan was to fly the ILS-9L at Opa Locka Airport (KOPF). When we arrived in the area a very large thunderstorm was sitting stationary on the final approach course about three miles from the airport. I suggested that we go to Ft. Lauderdale Executive Airport (KFXE) and do the ILS-8 approach.

The applicant said, "I don't have my approach book. It's back at the airport."

I asked, "What approaches do you have with you?"

He answered, "I only have the OPF ILS-9L approach plate. I thought that's what you wanted to do."

Why would an instructor of all people fly without his charts? He received a second Notice of Disapproval.

An applicant for Commercial Pilot AMEL was flying a Piper Seminole (PA-44). During the instrument phase of the flight test he was cleared for the, "Localizer 15 circle to land on Runway 28." at Pompano Beach Airpark (KPMP). The final approach fix is JIMNY located at 6.8 DME on the localizer. The applicant delayed his descent until he was at 5.8 DME where he extended the landing gear and selected flaps to 25 degrees. I thought this was interesting as we were flying the circling approach with a simulated engine failure and a better plan would have been to delay any flaps until lined up on final. Pompano Tower instructed him to "Enter a right downwind for Runway 28." At one mile from the airport I told the applicant to look outside and fly visually. He flew over Runway 15 and passed over the intersection of Runway 15 and Runway 28 continuing to the Southeast. I asked him what he was doing.

He replied, "Oh, I'm past the runway. He then started a right turn to head back to the airport but saw that he was not in position for a landing and decided to make a single engine go-around. During this maneuver he forgot to retract the landing gear and the flaps. During the debrief he explained his errors were the result of, "I never landed on Runway 28 before."

Another applicant for Commercial Pilot AMEL was cleared for the, "Localizer 15 circle to land on Runway 6." at KPMP. The approach was being flown with a simulated engine failure so the applicant selected gear down at JIMNY and said he would delay the flaps until on final. The Minimum Descent Altitude (MDA) on this circling approach is 660 feet MSL. The applicant descended to 500 feet MSL before leveling the airplane. When he went visual he entered an upwind leg for Runway 6 and flew that heading for about 30 seconds and then made a 270 degree right turn into a downwind for Runway 33. When asked what he was doing, the applicant replied, "I am lost."

An applicant for Commercial Pilot AMEL was flying a Cessna 414. He was cleared for the ILS-8R at North County Airport (F45). As he began intercepting the localizer he allowed the bank angle to reach 45 degrees. He was above glide-slope intercept altitude and began a descent that reached a rate of 2500 fpm. He drifted through the localizer and turned the other direction at a bank angle of 60 degrees. By now the descent rate had reached 3500 fpm. As my life's story began to replay before my eyes I took control of the aircraft. Amazingly, the applicant had no idea of the danger he had been in and said, "Why did I fail?"

Epilogue

I can't believe that this book is finished. Twenty one years of note keeping and seven years of writing, re-writing and editing. When progress slowed my wife, Lena, pushed me to continue. Without her believing in this project it might never have been finished.

What's ahead? As long as I can pass the flight physical and my POI (Principal Operations Inspector) sees fit to renew my designation, I will continue on as a DPE (Designated Pilot Examiner). How else could I meet such interesting people, fly the latest models of new aircraft and get paid for it! My wife says to start a new notebook for Volume 2. We'll see how it goes with Volume 1.

And a special thanks to all the people at Dorrance Publishing, who guided this project from a raw manuscript to the finished book you have thankfully purchased and I hope you are reading with enjoyment.

If we meet at an airport say hello. It would be fun to swap flying stories.